ALLENTOWN
Remembered
A Postcard History

Happy Memories
Myra J Outwater

Remember
& Enjoy

Robert B

Myra Yellin Outwater
and Robert Bungerz

ST. MICHAEL'S EVANGEL... ...N CHURCH

Centre Square and South Seventh Street,
showing Second National Bank Building.
Allentown, Pa.

SECOND NATIONAL BANK

PHOTOGRAPHERS.

Schiffer
Publishing Ltd

380 Lower Valley Road Atglen, Pennsylvania 19310

Dedication

To Eric Outwater
We thank you for your patience and encouragement, and
for believing that we could do anything.

To Allen Brandstein
Thank you for your patience, support, and for not mind-
ing all the time spent on this project.

Other Schiffer Books by Myra and Eric Outwater:
Floridiana
Florida Kitsch
Ocean Liner Memorabilia
Judaica
Garden Ornaments and Antiques
Garden Tools
Cast Iron Automotive Toys
Advertising Dolls

Copyright © 2007 by Myra Yellin Outwater
Library of Congress Control Number: 2007932594

Designed by John P. Cheek
Cover design by Bruce Waters
Type set in Novarese Bk BT/Zurich BT

ISBN: 978-0-7643-2750-6
Printed in China

Published by Schiffer Publishing Ltd.
4880 Lower Valley Road
Atglen, PA 19310
Phone: (610) 593-1777; Fax: (610) 593-2002
E-mail: Info@schifferbooks.com

For the largest selection of fine reference books on this and related subjects, please visit our web site at **www.schifferbooks.com**
We are always looking for people to write books on new and related subjects. If you have an idea for a book please contact us at the above address.

This book may be purchased from the publisher.
Include $3.95 for shipping.
Please try your bookstore first.
You may write for a free catalog.

In Europe, Schiffer books are distributed by
Bushwood Books
6 Marksbury Ave.
Kew Gardens
Surrey TW9 4JF England
Phone: 44 (0) 20 8392-8585; Fax: 44 (0) 20 8392-9876
E-mail: info@bushwoodbooks.co.uk
Website: www.bushwoodbooks.co.uk
Free postage in the U.K., Europe; air mail at cost.

Contents

INTERIOR VIEW, METROPOLE CAFE, 837 HAMILTON ST., ALLENTOWN, PA.   H. O. HAAS, PROP.

Acknowledgements

Our sincere thanks go to:

Glenn Koch, our long-distance advisor who, although now living in San Francisco, remains an Allentonian at heart and whose encouragement, enthusiasm and vast knowledge of Allentown history, people, and places were always just a phone call away

Ted Rosenberger and Kevin Sprague

Judith A. Harris, Esquire

Handy Dan for all his assistance

Dolly Yanolko, a friend and another collector of Allentown post cards

Dr. Ralph F. Merkle and Earlene C. Dech, booth deceased now, who encouraged Robert to start collecting Allentown postcards

All our friends who have already ordered copies of the book

The people of Allentown who have been so welcoming and constantly remind us what makes Allentown such a nice place to live

——ALL THE RAGE——
SOUVENIR CARDS
LARGEST VARIETY AND LOWEST PRICES
Cards of Allentown. Easton. Bethlehem. Glen Onoko, New York, and many prominent points
At SHAFER'S BOOK STORE, 33 N. 7th St., Allentown, Pa.

INTERIOR OF SHAFER'S BOOK STORE
Headquarters for Bibles, Albums, Artist. Wax and Paper Flower Material, Stationery, blank Books, S. S. and Church Supplies, &c.

Preface
Historic Images Through Postcards

Postcards are one of the most popular collectibles. The urge to horde them sprang up with the birth of this means of communication at the turn of the twentieth century and has endured great changes in the printing industry. Today, postcard shows take place every weekend somewhere in the country, or the world, and millions of pieces of ephemera lie in wait for those who collect obscure topics or town views.

Postcards once served as the email of their day. Beginning in the 1890s, they were the fastest, most popular means of communication in the United States. These timely cards provided a way to send scenes through the mail, along with brief messages–a way to enchant friends and family with the places travelers visited, to send local scenes, or to share favorite topics of imagery. They even provided the latest breaking news, as images of fires, floods, shipwrecks, and festivals were often available in postcard form within hours of an event. Moreover, mail delivery was received by most homes in the United States at least twice a day. So someone might send a morning postcard inviting a friend to dinner that evening, and receive an RSVP in time to shop for food.

The messages shared and the beautiful scenes combine to create the timeless appeal of postcards as a collectible. Most importantly, history is recorded by the pictures of the times, moments in time reflecting an alluring past.

Dating Postcards

Determining the ages of postcards, because of the specifics of the times, is not terribly difficult.

Pioneer Era (1893-1898): Most pioneer cards in today's collections begin with cards placed on sale at the Columbian Exposition in Chicago on May 1, 1893. These were illustrations on government printed postal cards and privately printed souvenir cards. The government cards had the printed one-cent stamp, while souvenir cards required a two-cent adhesive postage stamp to be applied. Writing was not permitted on the address side of the card.

Private Mailing Card Era (1898-1901): On May 19, 1898, private printers were granted permission, by an act of Congress, to print and sell cards that bore the inscription "Private Mailing Card." A one-cent adhesive stamp was required. A dozen or more American printers began to take postcards seriously. Writing was still not permitted on the back.

Post Card Era - Undivided Back (1901-1907): New U.S. postal regulations on December 24, 1901, stipulated that the words "Post Card" should be printed at the top of the address side of privately printed cards. Government-issued cards were to be designated as "Postal Cards." Writing was still not permitted on the address side. In this era, private citizens began to take black and white photographs and have them printed on paper with post card backs.

Early Divided Back Era (1907-1914): Postcards with a divided back were permitted in Britain in 1902, but not in the U.S. until March 1, 1907. The address was to be written on the right side; the left side was for writing messages. Many millions of cards were published in this era. Up to this point, most postcards were printed in Germany, which was far ahead of the United States in the use of lithographic processes. With the advent of World War I, the suppliers of postcards for American consumption switched from Germany to England and the United States.

White Border Era (1915-1930): Most United States postcards were printed during this period. To save ink, publishers left a clear border around the view, thus these postcards are referred to as "White Border" cards. The relatively high cost of labor, along with inexperience and changes in public taste, resulted in the production of poor quality cards during this period. Furthermore, strong competition in a narrowing market caused many publishers to go out of business.

Linen Era (1930-1944): New printing processes allowed printing on postcards with high rag content that created a textured finish. These cheap cards allowed the use of gaudy dyes for coloring.

Photochrome Era (1945 to date): "Chrome" postcards began to dominate the scene soon after the Union Oil Company placed them in its western service stations in 1939. Mike Roberts pioneered with his "WESCO" cards soon after World War II. Three-dimensional postcards also appeared in this era.

A pre-1920s photo card of a Wentz Memorial display at the Allentown Fair. This card can be easily dated because Wentz is using its pre-1920s address. This is also an example of a very desirable card because it fits into so many collecting categories. First it is a photo card of an old Allentown business. It is also a funeral card, and it is an Allentown Fair card. $75.

Postcards can be dated by the images on the card, such as women's or men's hairstyles or clothing, automobiles, buildings no longer in existence or by the printing process, the color process, and the price of the postage. Since the majority of the postcards in this book date from 1900 to 1920, postage due was one cent for domestic mail and two cents for foreign mail.

In the late nineteenth century and through the early 1900s, people sent out private mailing cards or photo cards either of their homes, their own portraits, or of other intimate family events. Photographs of community buildings were also commonly used as postal cards.

From 1907 through 1920, postcards had divided backs, with a separate section for the address and another for the message. From 1915-1930, postcards had a white border around the front image. Linen postcards were produced in the 1930s and continued to be manufactured through the mid-1940s. Chrome-colored postcards became popular in the 1950s, and "chrome glossy" postcards began circulating in the late 1950s-1960s.

Pricing and What Is It Worth?

In judging the quality and value of these postcards, it is important to remember that collectors collect as much for nostalgia as they do for history. Another rule in collecting is to always try to get the very best quality and condition possible. The value of worn or torn postcards always remains in the lower ranges of the value scale unless the image is rare.

Postcards that cross categories also have more value and are more collectible. For example there are general collectors and specialists. So a card of Dorney Park would be of interest to Allentown memorabilia collectors, and also amusement park collectors. If there was also an image of a carousel, then we would add carousel collectors to the mix. If it showed a clown, a penny arcade, an old railroad or a trolley, that also would add to its value since it would appeal to even more collectors on a national level.

All the postcards in this book are from the Robert Bungerz collection. Robert Bungerz will answer any inquiries about Allentown postcards and/or memorabilia; he can be reached at 610-248-9342.

Neither the authors nor the publisher are responsible for any outcome that may result from using this guide.

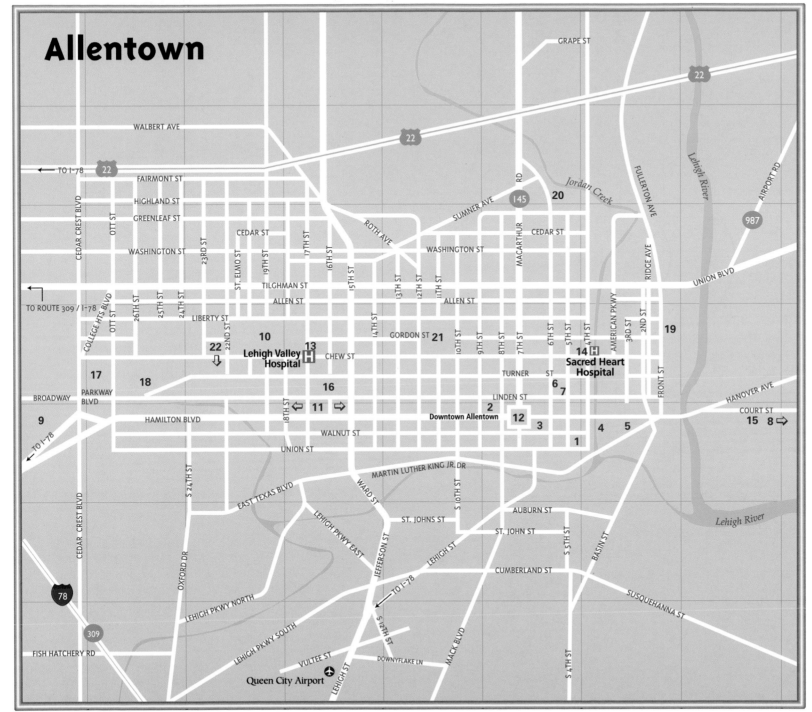

Allentown

1. Trout Hall
2. Hess Bros.
3. H. Leh
4. L. V. R. R. Station
5. C. N. J. R. R. Station
6. Orpheum Theater
7. Lyric Theater
8. Central Park
9. Dorney's Park
10. Allentown Fair Grounds
11. Millionaire's Row
12. Center Square
13. Allentown Hospital
14. Sacred Heart Hospital
15. State Hospital
16. West Park
17. Rose Garden
18. Cedar Parkway
19. Riverfront Park
20. Jordan Playground
21. West-Union Cemetery
22. Greenwood Cemetery

Map courtesy of the Lehigh Valley Convention and Visitors Bureau.

1. Allentown
An All-American City

One summer evening in 1964, my husband and I drove down from New York City to visit an old college friend in Easton, Pennsylvania. Since it was the weekend of the Great Allentown Fair, our hosts took us to Allentown.

The evening was clear and warm. The night was lit with neon lights. Spotlights crisscrossed the sky. There were loud and boisterous noises coming from all directions. Above us, the Ferris Wheel passengers were screaming with fear and delight. Around us, the sideshow barkers were hyping their menageries of human curiosities.

And as we walked up and down the midway, we watched the crowds fire rifles at moving water wheels, hoping to win goldfish or oversized stuffed animals. We watched them snack on sugared funnel cakes, french fried vegetables, waffles, ice cream, root beers, pretzels, and beer. And coming from the big city, we felt like aliens dropping in on a way of life we thought had long past.

Two years later, we moved to Allentown, refugees from the urban turbulence of New York in the 1960s. As we settled in, we saw the city of Allentown in a new light. Downtown streets were lined with rows of neatly kept Queen Anne style row houses, with detailed cornices topped with turreted and towered roofs. We saw women in aprons and head scarves outside sweeping their porch steps. And we saw streets curiously devoid of traffic jams.

Allentown, in the 1960s, was still a provincial, predominantly Pennsylvania German community. Before long, I learned the word "auslander." An *auslander* was someone who was not a native. I remember asking a new friend, a woman in her late forties, whether she was a native. "Oh, no," she answered very sincerely, "I was born in Tamaqua and didn't move to Allentown until I was nine months old."

Now, the Allentown fairgrounds were in the middle of my neighborhood and part of my daily landscape. Every day, as I passed them, I marveled at the long-gone city leaders who created this agricultural oasis in the middle of the city. The fairgrounds was across the street from the busy Allentown Hospital, in the midst of doctors' offices and emergency rooms, and close to the nearby William Allen High School.

Like many of my friends, I soon became a regular shopper at the Farmers' Market, held every weekend in the fairgrounds. Every Friday I would buy farm-fresh local produce, poultry, and meats. Like the rest of my neighbors, I would come to dread Fair Week, and each year at the end of the summer, I would plan my errands and shopping to avoid this week-long disruption of noise, traffic jams, and chaos.

Even as late as the 1970s, the Fair still celebrated its agricultural origins and the most popular attractions were livestock and animal displays, craft exhibitions, baking contests, and a silly clown named Dapper Dan who walked around tickling everyone's fancy with a rubber chicken. And there was Willie Restum, an Allentown native and big-time Las Vegas and Atlantic City entertainer, who would leave his home in Los Angeles to entertain his friends, family, and hometown audience on opening night with a show full of local nostalgia and never-forgotten Allentown school songs. Each year the Fair got full-page coverage each day from *The Morning Call* newspaper.

Shopping downtown was fun. Hamilton Street was lined with small, narrow shops where salespeople knew you by name and where you were sure to meet at least one or two friends. There was charm and elegance about these stores, with their ornate facades, and an Old World charm about the streets lined with tall lamp posts that were filled with garlands of seasonal flowers. Who could forget Hamilton Street's local "treasure," Hess' Department Store, which boasted an annual European fashion show, frequent Hollywood visitors, and another over-the-top extravaganza, the Hess Flower Show?

Before long, I was enjoying my new hometown's curious mix of eccentricities. Allentown was uniquely parochial. Its citizens were filled with pride about their own history and curiously disinterested in what was going on in the neighboring towns of Easton and Bethlehem, grateful they could keep their distance from the faster-moving worlds of New York and Philadelphia. People still told jokes in a strange dialect called Pennsylvania "Dutch" (a corruption of the word *Deutsch*) and Hess's Department Store made headlines with its constant parade of visiting celebrities and national leaders.

2. How It All Started
The History of Allentown

The story begins in 1735, when William Allen, a wealthy Philadel-phian, bought from his business associate, Joseph Turner, more than 5,000 acres of undeveloped woods and fields near the Lehigh River. Like many men of the time, Turner had received this land as payment from Thomas Penn, whose father, William Penn, was one of the larg-est landowners in the colonies. Since the Penns owned so much land, they often paid their business debts with land instead of cash.

Within a short time, Allen established permanent roots in the Lehigh Valley. In 1740, he built a small log cabin near the confluence of the Lehigh River and the Jordan Creek and named it Trout Hall, because of the abundance of trout in the nearby streams. For the next few years, Allen and his friends would travel from Philadelphia to hunt and fish at his lodge.

William Allen wanted to develop a town similar in design to Penn's Philadelphia. He mapped out his city, which he named Northampton-town, in a grid of forty-two city blocks. But Northamptontown became known as "Mr. Allen's little town," and in 1838 it was formally renamed Allentown.

William's third son, James, created the foundation of what we now know as the city of Allentown. James built a Georgian styled man-sion in the center of town in 1767 that he named Trout Hall, after his father's old fishing lodge.

Allen's mansion was considerably larger than the other homes in the area and reflected English architecture of the day. When com-pleted, Trout Hall was a two-and-a-half story stone house with a sym-metrical floor plan and floor space of forty feet on each side of the home. The southeast and northwest facades had five large windows and doors. The south facade was built with sandstone imported from the Philadelphia area. The other walls were built of native, hard, blue limestone and were laid out in what is now known as the irregular German style.

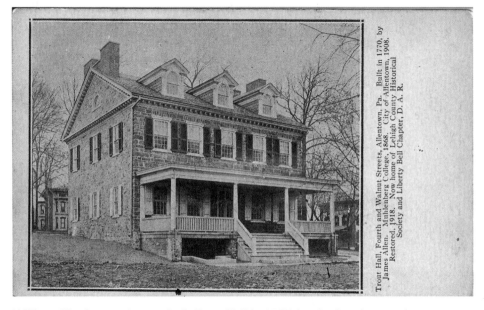

Trout Hall, Fourth and Walnut Streets, Allentown, Pa. Built in 1770, by James Allen. Muhlenberg College, 1868. City of Allentown, 1908. Restored, 1918. Now home of Lehigh County Historical Society and Liberty Bell Chapter, D. A. R.

William Allen's son, James, built Trout Hall in 1767, but in the nineteenth century the house changed owners many times and each new owner added architectural additions. Today the house has been returned to its original design, and extras, such as this porch, have been removed. $15.

When the Allens moved into their home in 1770, they became known for their gracious hospitality. Trout Hall became one of the most popular colonial gathering places outside of Philadelphia, and for the next seventy-five years its owners set the social standards for the community.

Allentown was situated on the King's Highway, the main route between New York and Philadelphia. As travelers journeyed back and forth between the two major cities, they would stop at Trout Hall and visit the Allens, who had become an influential colonial group related through marriage to many of the leading families in the American colonies.

Revolutionary stirrings in Philadelphia impacted the Allens, who remained Tories steadfast in their loyalty to the English King. When the Revolutionary War broke out in June of 1776, the Allens left Allentown in self-imposed exile. James Allen died a few months later, at the age of 36 years.

In 1794, James's daughter Margaret and her husband, William Tilghman, moved back to Trout Hall and reestablished the Allen legacy. James's other daughter, Anne Penn Greenleaf, and her husband also returned and built their own large home at the corner of Fifth and Hamilton Streets. When the Tilghmans died, Walter Livingston and his wife, Mary, moved into Trout Hall and lived there from 1825 to 1845. During this time, the Allen homestead became known as Livingston Hall.

After the Livingstons died, Trout Hall was leased to the Allentown Seminary, which remained there until 1864. Then the home was rented to the Allentown Collegiate Institute and Military Academy. In 1868 the Lutheran Church bought the property and established a new Lutheran affiliated school, Muhlenberg College.

In 1905, Muhlenberg College moved to its present location on Chew Street, in the newly developing West End. The City of Allentown bought the Trout Hall property. In 1916 there was a serious campaign to raise funds to restore the house to its eighteenth century design, by eliminating nineteenth century architectural additions.

Today, Trout Hall is owned by the Lehigh County Historical Society. It is listed on the National Register of Historic Places and is Allentown's best-known historic landmark.

From Farm to City

Geography and natural resources made Allentown a desirable place to settle. Farmers came because of its rich and fertile land. Merchants, coal miners, and factory owners were attracted by its access to the Lehigh River and its proximity to the ports of New York and Philadelphia.

Allentown was downstream from the Pennsylvania coal regions. Throughout the nineteenth century, coal was transported by the Lehigh Coal and Navigation Company (LCNC) to out-of-state markets. By the 1830s and 1840s, the Lehigh Valley was experiencing its own industrial revolution, thanks to its canal system and newly expanding railroad network.

In 1822 the Lehigh Coal and Navigation Company was handling over 2,240 tons of coal. A year later, this amount had doubled. By 1855, over 1,275, 000 tons of coal were transported downstream. Canal traffic reached its heyday in the 1850s, but coal was not the only commodity shipped downstream. Barges also carried lumber, flour, whiskey, limestone, and iron, as well as a heavy passenger trade. Floods in 1862 caused major damage to the Canal system, but the canals were rebuilt and continued to flourish until floods of 1901 and 1904 closed the upper reaches of the canal, seriously impacting the system's efficiency. But by then there was already a flourishing rail system, and Allentown continued to be a successful marketing hub connecting the coal regions with Philadelphia and New York markets.

It was logical that young Allentonians would see new opportunities, leave family farms, and head to the cities, where there were jobs opening in the silk mills, saw mills, iron foundries, cement mills, breweries, and cigar factories. As these industries grew more widespread and flourished, Allentown was transformed from a farm to an industrial society.

Part of the new growth stemmed from the influx of immigrants who brought a new and willing labor force to the area. For most of the nineteenth century, the dominant ethnic group in Allentown had been people of German stock, who maintained their Old World customs and even conducted their business in the German language. In the 1870s, 1880s, and 1890s, European immigrants—such as Irish, Italian, Eastern European Jewish, Polish, Russian, and later Syrian and Lebanese people moved into the old neighborhoods; Allentown truly became a melting pot.

And as the population shifted from the downtown to new neighborhoods developing beyond the city's original western boundaries, Allentown's new monied class bought spacious lots and began to build larger, grander, and more architecturally opulent homes.

World War I impacted the area dramatically, as subsequent anti-German sentiments grew, making the local people self-conscious about their German roots. Many locals stopped speaking German in public; English became the dominant language and the Pennsylvania German dialects were used only at home.

This book concentrates on the period that today we call Allentown's Golden Age, the late 1890s through the 1950s. During this period, downtown Hamilton Street became a smart shopping street with quality stores, elegant hotels, restaurants, legitimate theatres, vaudeville, and silent and talkie movie houses.

3. Hamilton Street Stores

The nineteenth and twentieth centuries witnessed major changes in downtown shopping patterns. In the years following the end of the Civil War, stores began to emerge along Hamilton Street, filled with sewing goods and notions, sporting goods, china, jewelry, groceries, men's and women's clothing, shoes, furs, and hats. As young men left their families' farms and moved to the city, a new merchant class emerged, eager to make their fortunes.

Philadelphian John Wanamaker had revolutionized the region's retail market. In 1876, he established the first department store in America. Before long, the idea of selling a variety of goods caught on elsewhere. Shops began to advertise different "departments" in their stores, each offering a variety of related goods.

The idea of selling pre-made, store-bought, ready-to-wear clothing was another innovation of the late nineteenth century. While pre-made was not a new idea to wealthy women who often ordered their clothes from New York, London, and Paris fashion houses (and even went to Europe to buy special gowns and dresses), it was a new concept for the average American woman, who either made her own clothes and those of her children or hired a seamstress to make clothes for the family.

Hess Brothers Department Store

Hess Brothers, which would become the best known of Allentown's department stores, was established by chance. Brothers Charles and Max Hess had come to Allentown from Perth Amboy, New Jersey. They noticed that the Grand Central Hotel had a vacant store front, and in 1897 they set up the Hess Brothers Dry Goods Store there, on the first floor, at 831 Hamilton Street. Within a few years, the store had expanded into the entire first floor of the hotel. By the 1920s, it occupied the hotel's entire five stories.

Max Hess's son, Max Hess, Jr., further expanded the store by taking over the entire block. He bought or leased all the neighboring properties in the 800 block of Hamilton Street, and by the early 1940s

the business, now known just as Hess's, extended to the corner of Ninth and Hamilton Streets.

Street frontage was always expensive on Hamilton Street and the price of real estate was the reason that the stores occupied such narrow spaces. In fact, because the stores were dark and narrow, their early owners frequently added skylights in the ceilings to provide more light.

But the high price of real estate didn't discourage Max Hess, Jr., whose goal was to expand the store; money was not an obstacle. When he bought the final piece of property on Hamilton Street, he astounded everyone by paying the highest price-per-foot that had ever been paid for street frontage. It remained a record price until 1955, when the newly formed First National Bank bought the old Hotel Allen-Koch Brothers property.

Once Hess acquired the last of the Hamilton Street properties, he gave the store a face lift by uniting all the fronts into a larger and more streamlined façade. He also changing the store name and the signage.

Max Hess's marketing strategies were legendary; he brought glitz to Allentown. Hess understood human psychology and knew that it was important to keep shoppers inside the store; when they left, he lost their potential purchasing power. Therefore, he opened the Patio Restaurant to serve lunches and early dinners. He offered a menu that served large portions, deluxe specials, gigantic cocktails, and daily entertainment, such as Hess models showing off the latest fashions. The menu offered birthday specials for adults and children. Hess's famous strawberry pie was piled so high with strawberries and whipped cream that many local hostesses served them at their own dinner parties.

Hess also introduced the annual Hess's Flower Shows, runway fashion shows, the movie stars, and paid for frequent appearances of famous guests who became magnets for shoppers outside the Allentown area. At Christmas time, there was an annual "Pip the Mouse" Christmas show, that soon became a favorite family activity. Hess's windows were filled with giant German toys and automated figures, some of which cost upwards of ten thousand dollars. He also hung expensive and elaborate crystal chandeliers on the first floor and displayed expensive antiques and "objets d'art" along the escalators.

In his book, *Every Dollar Counts*, Hess explained that it was important to locate the "up" escalators as far away as possible from the "down" escalators, so that customers had to walk through each of the shopping floors. This same reasoning prompted him to place tables with sale items near the entrance to the Patio Restaurant, to entice the eye and interest of shoppers waiting in line to enter the restaurant.

Hess was very competitive. If he saw a Hamilton Street competitor selling an item at a discount, he immediately advertised that Hess's was selling it for even less, believing that he would make up the difference in future sales.

In 1965, Hess called upon a local entrepreneur, Philip Berman, and offered to sell him Hess's. Berman, who had recently retired from the Berman Brothers Trucking Business, was intrigued. Berman paid Max Hess more than $16 million dollars in cash. Years later, Berman recalled that he had only spoken to Max Hess twice in his life: once when Hess asked him if he wanted to buy Hess's, and the other the day he finalized the sale. Max Hess died soon afterward, never enjoying a retirement.

Berman, like Hess, was a natural showman. He hired Max Rosey, formerly a New York and Broadway press agent, to capitalize on the notoriety Max Hess had created. At the time, Rosey had one other client: Nathan's Famous Coney Island hot dogs. Rosey, together with Berman, worked to keep Hess's store in both the local and the national limelight. Berman invited stars, as well as national politicians and leaders, to be his guest at the store.

The French Room, begun in 1907 by the Hess Brothers, continued to be a Hess tradition through the early 1980s. Originally, it was a women's salon specializing in quality undergarments and clothing. By the 1960s, it was selling exclusive French and Italian runway fashions, and it was rumored that movie stars such as Elizabeth Taylor shopped at Hess's. In the 1980s, when the French artist Francoise Gilot, a former mistress of Pablo Picasso and a close friend of Muriel Berman (Phil's wife), married Jonas Salk, the man who developed the Salk polio vaccine, she bought her wedding dress at Hess's.

Hess's store remained a downtown landmark and symbol of Allentown's prosperity until it was torn down in the early twenty-first century, to make way for a new Pennsylvania Power and Light office building complex.

H. Leh & Company

The H. Leh & Company store dates back to the 1850s, when young Henry Leh left his family's farm and set up a shoe manufacturing company in downtown Allentown. Within a few years, he founded Henry Leh's Lion's Clothing Hall, which had a large figure of a lion in front. In 1860, he established H. Leh & Company, which became one of Allentown's most popular stores. When it closed in the late 1990s, H. Leh & Company had the distinction of being the oldest business on Hamilton Street.

Retailing seemed to run in the Koch family. Horatio B. Koch married Henry Leh's daughter, Sallie, and soon became a partner in Leh's Department Store. His brothers, Frank and Thomas, opened Koch Brothers, a men's clothing store, on the main floor of the Hotel Allen, on the northeast corner of Center Square and Hamilton Street. Years later, in 1955, the newly formed First National Bank bought this property.

Their nephew, Will Koch, opened his own store at the corner of Center Square. Originally known as the Stillwagon Store, the new Koch store was later named Koch & Person. When Person retired, the store became the Will Koch Clothing store. It survived through 1920, when its building was demolished in order to build the new Merchants Bank, which was completed in 1921.

Hinterleiter Dry Goods Store

The Hinterleiter Dry Goods Store, at 635 Hamilton Street, sold yard goods, patterns, sewing goods, bolts of cloth, buttons, patterns, and zippers as well as ready-made clothing outfits.

Anewalt Brothers

The Anewalt Brothers owned three different stores: Anewalt Brothers, at 615 Hamilton Street; Lewis Anewalt, at 617 Hamilton Street; and S. B. Anewalt, which was at the corner of Eighth and Hamilton Streets, next to M.S. Young Hardware store. All three stores sold hats and, later, furs.

The Anewalt Brothers' store was distinguished in the memories of old-time Allentonians by the presence of a large, white bear figure standing out front. The Lewis Anewalt store had a brown bear in front. When Anewalt Brothers' closed, the white bear was moved upstairs in a building on North Seventh Street.

The two Anewalt bears, along with an eight-foot-high white rabbit, that stood outside Haas's Metropole Café, and H. Leh's lion, were often referred to affectionately as "the Hamilton Street menagerie."

Other well-known names among Allentown's downtown merchants included Zollinger, Earley, Farr, Wetherhold, Metzger, W. H. Appel, and Keller.

The Hess Brothers eventually took over the entire Grand Central Hotel. $15

Hess Brothers is probably the most famous of all the Allentown department stores due to the charismatic personalities and showmanship of two men, Max Hess, Jr. and Philip Berman, whose sense of showmanship made shopping at Hess' an adventure. $10.

Hess Brothers opened for business on the first floor of the Grand Central Hotel. Later it expanded and eventually the Hesses bought the entire store and soon boasted that its first floor extended five stories with a roof rotunda. $10.

Henry Leh founded H. Leh & Company in 1860. The store survived into the twentieth century, and when it finally closed in the late 1990s, it was the oldest continuing business on Hamilton Street. $15.

The coat department at H. Leh & Company. $10.

Hinterleiter's Department Store-First Floor, 635 Hamilton Street, Allentown, Pa. Our Large Ready-to-Wear Dept. on Second Floor.

A view of the interior of Hinterleiter's. $5.

Koch Brothers, one of Allentown's best known men's clothiers, was located on the main floor of the Hotel Allen, on the Northeast corner of Center Square. In 1955 the site was bought by the newly formed First National Bank. $10.

FALL AND WINTER STYLES NOW READY AT
KOCH BROS.
TOWN'S LEADING CLOTHIERS & FURNISHERS

DEPARTMENT STORE HINTERLEITER'S 635 HAMILTON ST. ALLENTOWN.

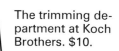

KOCH BROTHERS TRIMMING AND TAILORING ROOMS

The trimming department at Koch Brothers. $10.

A photo card of a billboard of the Hinterleiter Department store, a small dry goods store at 635 Hamilton Street which sold yard goods, patterns and sewing goods. The store sold ready to wear on the second floor. $15.

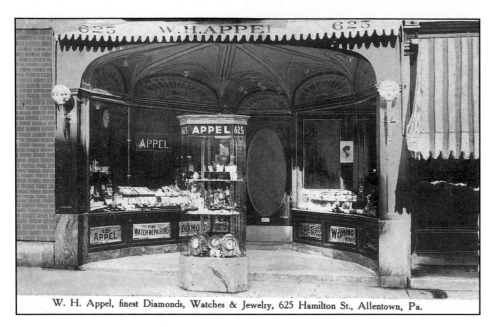

W. H. Appel, finest Diamonds, Watches & Jewelry, 625 Hamilton St., Allentown, Pa.

W. H. Appel Jeweler was established in 1865 at 623 Hamilton Street, and later expanded to 625 Hamilton Street. When Appel Jeweler closed its doors in 2002, it was the last of the old Hamilton Street businesses. $20.

W. H. Appel, finest Diamonds, Watches & Jewelry, 625 Hamilton St., Allentown, Pa.

The interior of the store. $10.

14806   Jewelery Store of E. Keller & Sons, Allentown, Pa.

E. Keller & Sons was founded in 1865 at 711 Hamilton Street, and until it closed its doors in the late 1920s, it was considered the best jewelry store in Allentown. $10.

F. S. Musselman Jeweler at 22 North Sixth Street. $15.

The Will H. Koch Clothing Store, on the southwestern corner of Center Square, was originally the Stillwagon Store. It became Koch & Person. When Person left, it was renamed the Will H. Koch Clothing Store. This building was sold in 1920 to the Merchants Bank. $50.

Faust & Landes Jeweler at 728 Hamilton Street. $15.

Breinig and Bachman,
Clothiers & Furnishers.
Sixth & Hamilton Streets,
Allentown, Pa.

THE "NEW WAY" CLOTHING STORE, BREINIG & BACHMAN CO., SIXTH AND HAMILTON STS. ALLENTOWN, PA.

The interior of Breinig &
Bachman. $15.

Breinig & Bachman, Tailors, Clothiers, and Haberdashers,
was located at the southeast corner of Sixth and Hamilton
Streets. $15.

The Hcinz Store at 808-814 Hamilton Street sold ladies' apparel. $30.

Nathan & Schatenstein Dry Goods Store at 519 /521 Hamilton Street. $15.

The millinery department at Heinz's. $25.

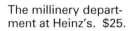

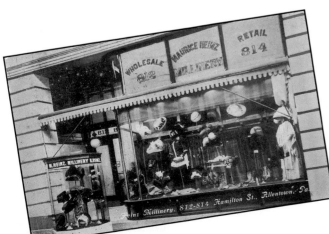

The old façade of the Heinz store. $25.

The Star Clothing Company at 714 Hamilton Street. There is a partial view of the Victor Theatre on the right of the Star Clothing building. $30.

The Ladies Department at Nathan & Schatenstein Dry Goods Store. $15.

The interior of the Star Clothing Company. $20.

The Lewis Anewalt Store at 617 Hamilton Street sold only hats. This store had a brown bear standing in front. $25.

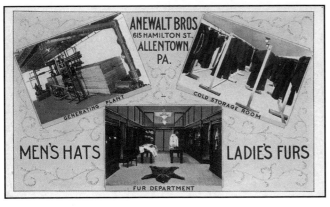

Anewalt Brothers' store, at 615 Hamilton Street, was the largest fur store in Allentown and was known for the large white bear standing outside its door. $45.

Another view of the Anewalt Brothers' store. The original Anewalt brothers, Samuel and John, grew tobacco in a field at North Seventh and Allen Streets which in 1886 would become the site of the future Pioneer Silk Mill. $15.

Farr Brothers & Co., at Eighth and Hamilton Streets, was one of the best known shoe stores in town and remained in business until 1986. $20.

The new facade of Farr's. $30.

The children's shoe department at Farr's. $20.

The next two Wetherhold & Metzger post cards were part of a set of six cards that were packaged in this envelope. $40

The children's shoe department at Wetherhold & Metzger. $10.

THE CHILDREN'S DEPARTMENT

WETHERHOLD & METZGER, 719 HAMILTON ST., ALLENTOWN, PA.

Kuhn's & Kerschner at 721 Hamilton Street. $10.

KUHNS & KERSCHNER

721

KUHNS & KERSCHNER NEW STORE FRONT, ALLENTOWN, PA. BENJ. F. KUHNS, PROP.

THE WETHERHOLD & METZGER SHOE & OFFICE BUILDING.

FAMOUS SHOES
WETHERHOLD & METZGER

WETHERHOLD & METZGER, 719 HAMILTON ST., ALLENTOWN, PA.
"THE STORE OF FAMOUS SHOES."   116701

Wetherhold & Metzger, at 719 Hamilton Street, was another popular shoe store. It left the downtown in the early 1980s. $15.

MEN'S AND BOYS' CLOTHIERS, FURNISHERS AND HATTERS.

BOHLEN GROSS & MOYER

721

BOHLEN, GROSS & MOYER, 721 HAMILTON ST., ALLENTOWN, PA.

Bohlen, Gross & Moyer at 721 Hamilton Street was the successor to Kuhns & Kerschner. The new store used the same post cards but inserted their new name. $10.

4. Other Businesses

By the late 1890s, business was thriving in downtown Allentown where merchants established grocery stores, music shops, cigar shops, florists, pharmacies, and bakeries. On the side streets, there were garages and showrooms catering to the carriage and newly developing automobile trade. There were also feed stores and new factories.

The Adelaide Silk Ribbon Mill was founded in 1881 on the northeast corner of Third and Linden Streets. The Pioneer Silk Mill was founded in 1886, at North Seventh and Allen Streets, in a field where two of the Anewalt Brothers used to grow tobacco.

For most of the nineteenth century, Nathan Martin's home on the southwest corner of Ninth and Hamilton Streets was a local landmark, until it was torn down in the 1960s. The New York Floral Company moved into a part of 906-912 Hamilton Street property. The old Allentown Free Library moved to the property also, but in the 1980s Philip Berman and Donald Miller, the publisher of the *Morning Call* newspapers, along with a group of other concerned businessmen, formed a partnership to build a new hotel to attract convention business. They also sought to upgrade the slowly disintegrating downtown. The Library moved to a new site at Twelfth and Hamilton Streets, and the New York Floral Company moved inside the lobby of the new hotel.

Throughout the nineteenth and twentieth centuries, it was common for cities to have multiple newspapers, with morning as well as afternoon editions. Allentown had three leading newspapers: *The Chronicle and News*, *The Daily City Item*, and the *Evening Leader*, all with evening editions, and readers who lived primarily in the city. The *Morning Call* was the only morning newspaper in the area. The *Allentown Democrat* was a weekly paper and was popular in rural areas of the county, as were the German newspapers, the *Lehigh Register*, the *Friedensbote*, the *Weltbote*, and the *Republicana*.

Allentown's oldest newspaper, the *Chronicle and News* dated back to the 1870s. In 1887, another longtime newspaper, *The Critic*, folded and was sold at a sheriff's sale to the then-mayor, Werner K. Ruhe. In 1895, David Miller, who had worked at *The Critic* while a student at Muhlenberg College, bought a quarter share of the merged newspaper, which was now renamed *The Morning Call*.

From 1894 to 1899, *The Morning Call* was published in a building at the southwest corner of Sixth and Walnut Streets. But in 1899, Miller bought the American Hose Company Building at 16 South Sixth Street and moved the newspaper's operations to it. *The Morning Call* stayed there until 1906, when it moved across the street to 27 South Sixth Street.

The Democrat and *The Daily City Item* newspapers were owned by George Hardner and headquartered in the Allentown Democrat Building on the northeastern corner of North Sixth and Linden Streets, near the present site of *The Morning Call*. In November, 1919, Hardner sold these two newspapers to a consortium of businessmen, including C.J. Smith, Peter Leisenring, Royal Weiler, Major J.C. Shumberger, and General Harry Trexler, and the new newspaper was renamed *The Morning Herald*. The following March, David and Samuel Miller, by now the sole owners of *The Morning Call*, sold *The Call* to this group, and the operations of all these newspapers were consolidated under the name, *The Morning Call*.

In that same year, the *Evening Item* was sold to *The Chronicle and News*, which was owned by Martin Kern, who also owned Daufers' Breweries. In 1921, the *Sunday Morning Call*, the area's first Sunday edition, came into being.

David Miller decided to go back into the newspaper business in 1934, and he bought back *The Morning Call*. In 1935 he and his new partners purchased *The Chronicle and News* and set up all the newspaper operations in the Sixth and Linden Street building. Eventually, the Miller family took complete control of *The Morning Call* and the *Evening Chronicle*, and for many years they ran them as separate newspapers, one as a morning paper and the other an evening edition.

During those years, *The Call* and *The Chronicle* occupied the same building. *The Morning Call* was on one side of the building and *The Evening Chronicle* was on the other side, and although they used the same facilities and printing presses, they acted as though they were competitors. Throughout the 1960s, 1970s, and 1980s, it was common for *Morning Call* reporters and *Evening Chronicle* reporters to compete for "scoops."

By the late twentieth century, changing economics and a decline in newspaper readership made afternoon and evening newspapers economically unfeasible. In the 1980s the two newspapers merged into *The Morning Call*.

In the 1980s, Donald Miller appointed his son Edward to be publisher of the newspaper. Edward Miller began to modernize the paper and introduce new technology. Gradually, computers and "pods" replaced typewriters and desks, and each night, after the newspaper went to bed and the staff left, a few more typewriters were spirited away. After a few difficult months, during which veteran newsmen threatened to quit if their typewriters were taken away, the newsroom was computerized and the newspaper began to produce new "magazine" sections along with the news.

After sharp disagreement with his son about the new direction of the newspaper and its emphasis on national rather than local coverage, Donald Miller approached Otis Chandler, of *The Los Angeles Times,* at a newspaper convention. Miller offered to sell Chandler *The Morning Call*, which was then one of the most profitable daily newspapers in the country. Chandler accepted the offer and *The Morning Call* was bought by the Times-Mirror Corporation. Today, the newspaper is for sale again.

Diehl's Furniture Store at 220-224 North Eighth Street. $10.

The main floor of Diehl's. $25.

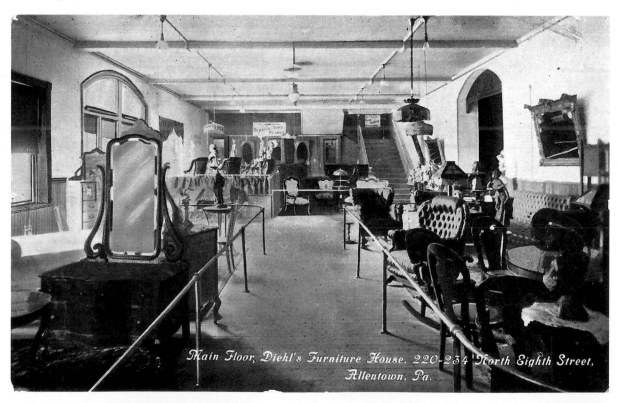

Diehl's Furniture House, 220-234 North Eighth Street, Allentown, Pa.

Main Floor, Diehl's Furniture House, 220-234 North Eighth Street, Allentown, Pa.

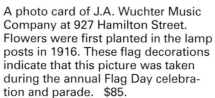

The grand piano department at Kramer's Music House. $25.

A photo card of J.A. Wuchter Music Company at 927 Hamilton Street. Flowers were first planted in the lamp posts in 1916. These flag decorations indicate that this picture was taken during the annual Flag Day celebration and parade. $85.

Kramer's Music House at 544 Hamilton Street. $60.

Minnich's Bakery at Turner and Madison Streets. $25.

The Chocolate Shop at 1109 Hamilton Street was owned by Harvey Haas who also owned the Metropole Café. $25.

THE NEW CHOCOLATE SHOP, 1109 HAMILTON ST., ALLENTOWN, PA.

The Smoker's Paradise at 732 Hamilton Street. $75.

Martin H. Strauss Wholesale Groceries at 114-118 South Second Street. $25.

Say it with Flowers.

JOHN F. HORN & BRO., 32 NORTH 6TH ST., ALLENTOWN, PA.

John Horn & Brothers Florist at 32 North Sixth Street. $35.

CONSERVATORY VIEW
NEW YORK FLORAL CO
ALLENTOWN, PA.

DISPLAY ROOM

The New York Floral at 906-912 Hamilton Street was located on the southwest corner of Ninth and Hamilton Streets on part of the site of the former Nathan Martin home. The Allentown Free Library was also located just west of here until the 1980s, when the library moved to Jefferson and Hamilton Streets. A new Hilton Hotel was built on this corner, and the New York Floral moved inside the lobby of the new hotel. $10.

Allentown Feb 3 1906

MERKLE & CO

Friend
Please ship 1 case
B. M. Coffee
To
M & Co

Merkle & Company Grocery was located on the southeastern corner of Eighth and Chew Streets. $45.

27

The Allentown Crockery at 37-39 South Seventh Street sold china, cut glass and silver. $15.

The exterior of Brown's White City Laundry. $40.

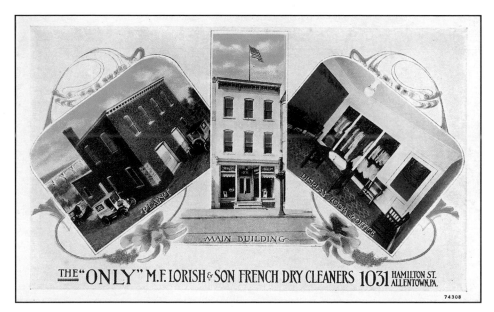

The Only Cleaners at 1031 Hamilton Street. $10.

Brown's White City Laundry at 126-128 North Tenth Street. $30.

Star Cleaners at 25 North Tenth Street. $35.

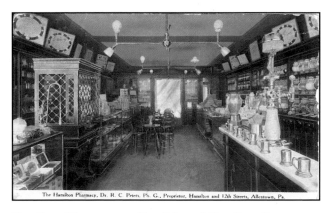

Hamilton Pharmacy at Twelfth and Hamilton Streets. $45.

Henry E. Peters Druggist at 639 Hamilton Street. $35.

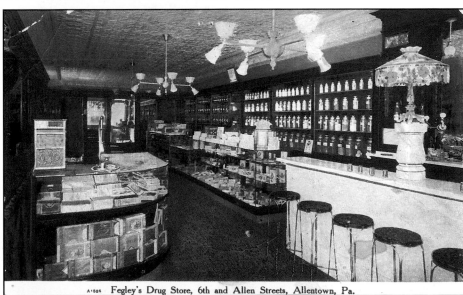

Fegley's Drug Store at Sixth and Allen Streets. $45.

ALLENTOWN'S FIRE PROOF STAG HOTEL AND NEW HOME OF "THE AMERICAN MEDICINE CO.."

THE WAIDELICH BUILDING, HAMILTON AT CHURCH ST., ALLENTOWN, PA.

"THE AMERICAN MEDICINE CO." YOUR REXALL STORE.

IN THE WAIDELICH BUILDING, HAMILTON AT CHURCH ST., ALLENTOWN, PA.

The interior of the American Medicine Company. $10.

The American Medicine Company occupied the first floor of the Waidelich Building at 627-629 Hamilton Street. The Stag Hotel, which opened in 1926, occupied the upper floors. The Stag Hotel remained a men's only hotel until 1932 when women were allowed to be guests. After Prohibition was repealed, the Subway Grille opened in the basement of the building. $10.

FLAT - IRON Store   Opp. Central Park
Allentown, Pa.

The Flatiron Store was located opposite Central Park in east Allentown on the border of Allentown and Bethlehem. This building still exists today. $100.

DISPLAY ROOMS, LEHIGH VALLEY SUPPLY CO., 926 HAMILTON ST., ALLENTOWN, PA.   111803

The Lehigh Valley Supply Company at 926 Hamilton Street. $10.

The Allentown Democrat Building at Sixth and Linden Streets housed both the Democrat and the Daily City Item newspapers. Today this site is the home of Allentown's only newspaper, the Morning Call. $15.

Democrat and Item Building, Allentown, Pa.

Flower Stands, Allentown, Pa.   A2

The P. P. and L. building, seen in the background, was built in 1928, and was Allentown's tallest building. It still is. In the foreground is one of the down town lamp posts that, beginning in 1916, were always filled with seasonal flowers. The then Mayor Reichenbach was inspired by his trip to Vienna and introduced the idea of putting flowers in the light posts to beautify the downtown. These floral lamp posts became the symbol of downtown Allentown. $5.

5. Hotels

George Savitz established the first Allentown hotel, the Compass and Square, at Center Square in 1801. In 1886, the Hotel Allen was built on the same site. The Hotel Allen was for many years considered one of Allentown's best hotels, hosting prominent city visitors such as Theodore Roosevelt, who visited Allentown several times and always stayed at the Hotel Allen. The hotel was torn down in the 1950s and replaced by the First National Bank.

The Eagle Hotel was another early Allentown establishment and the site of the farewell dinner for the Allentown Militia heading to Washington, D. C. to help President Lincoln fight the Civil War. A newspaper account of the day noted that, as a parting gift, each soldier was given a five-dollar note and a box of clothing, presumably their uniforms.

The Black Bear Hotel also served the city until it was razed in the 1890s, when Victor Barner bought the property and built the Grand Central Hotel. Here in 1897, the Hess Brothers rented the first floor for their original Hess Brothers Dry Goods Store. In the 1940s, when Max Hess, Jr., expanded Hess's to the corner of Ninth Street, the Grand Central Hotel and its neighbors were swallowed up in the grander Hess Brothers' façade.

The Columbia Hotel was built in the mid-nineteenth century at Tenth and Hamilton Street. It was bought by Martin Kern in 1915 when he also bought Daufers' Breweries. In that era, it was a common practice for breweries to own the local hotels and bars. Soon, the Columbia Hotel's original non-descript, flat-fronted façade and its interior were redesigned to resemble a German Beer Hall.

When the Columbia Hotel was torn down in 1929, its new owners had planned to build a modern building. Although the ground had been excavated, the economic downturn of the Depression put an end to construction plans. The lot remained empty until the late 1940s. when it was absorbed by a new "Park and Shop" downtown parking plan.

Other downtown hotels included the Hotel Penn on the northeast corner of North Seventh and Linden Streets, the Hotel Lenox at 34-36 North Eighth Street, and the City Hotel at 28-30 North Seventh Street. The Lafayette Hotel at 133-137 North Seventh Street, formerly known as the Black Horse Tavern, fell victim to another common problem in those days, fire. Like many of the downtown buildings, the hotel's construction was flammable, and the Lafayette burned down on January 23, 1926, in one of the worst fires in downtown Allentown's history.

Other hotels became local service clubs and organizations. The Hotel Walton, at the southeastern corner of North Eighth Street and Tilghman Streets, is now home to the West End Republican Club.

Many hotels existed outside the downtown Allentown area. The Fairgrounds Hotel was established in 1904 near the Fairgrounds. Central Park had the Manhattan Hotel, and Dorney Park had the Dorney Park Hotel. In 1917, after the Allentown College for Women vacated Fourth and Turner Streets, the former college buildings were purchased by the Gomery Brothers and converted into the College Hotel. This hotel burned down in 1939.

When the Hotel Traylor opened in 1917 at Fifteenth and Hamilton Streets, it was viewed by its neighbors as the first commercial intrusion in the new residential development on western Hamilton Street. However, its modern amenities, including the sky roof garden and lounge, soon made it a popular gathering place.

For many years the American Hotel stood on the corner of Sixth and Hamilton Streets, near Center Square. When the building was torn down in 1926, Albert Gomery, of Gomery Grocers, and other partners built the Americus Hotel there at a cost of $2.5 million. The name honored Amerigo Vespucci, the Italian explorer credited as the first man to step foot in America. When the Americus Hotel opened in 1928 with great fanfare, it brought elegance to Allentown's downtown area. The hotel continued to be a landmark for many years. By the late 1980s, despite attempts to renovate it, the hotel fell into decay and today is an under-utilized downtown space.

Hotel Allen, Monument Square,
Allentown, Pa.
The oldest dining place in
Lehigh County.

The Hotel Allen opened in 1891 on the northeast corner of Center Square and for many years it was considered one of Allentown's best hotels. Theodore Roosevelt was a guest here. The hotel was torn down in 1950s and replaced by the new First National Bank. $15.

City Hotel, Allentown, Pa.

The City Hotel at 28-30 North Seventh Street. $25.

13532 Main Lobby and Exchange in Hotel Allen, Allentown, Pa.

The lobby of the Hotel Allen. $10.

Main Office, City Hotel, Allentown, Pa.

The business office of the City Hotel. $20.

33

The dining room of the Hotel Columbia. $15.

CORNER OF MAIN DINING ROOM, HOTEL COLUMBIA, ALLENTOWN, PA.

Hotel Columbia, Tenth and Hamilton Sts., Allentown, Pa.

The bar at the Hotel Columbia. $45.

BAR AND LUNCH COUNTER, HOTEL COLUMBIA, HAMILTON and 10TH STREETS, ALLENTOWN, PA. ED. E. FENSTERMACHER

The Hotel Columbia, at Tenth and Hamilton Streets, was torn down in 1929 to make way for a new skyscraper. Although the ground was excavated, the Depression put a halt to these building plans and the lot remained empty until the 1950s when the land was absorbed by the "Park and Shop" and it became a parking lot for downtown shoppers. $20.

The Rathskeller in the Hotel Columbia. The Columbia Hotel was owned by Martin Kern who owned Daufer's Breweries and redesigned the building to look like a German Beer Hall. $25.

RATHSKELLER, HOTEL COLUMBIA, ALLENTOWN, PA.

Lafayette Hotel, Guth Bros. Prop's
133—137 North 7th Street,
Allentown, Pa.

The Lafayette Hotel
at 133-137 North
Seventh Street.
$15.

HOTEL WALTON.— A. O. WALT, PROPRIETOR.

The Hotel Walton, located
on the southeastern corner
of North Eighth and Tilghman Streets, is now the
home of the West End
Republican Club. $30

6594   DINING ROOM, LAFAYETTE HOTEL, ALLENTOWN, PA.

THE NEW HOTEL PENN, NORTH 7TH STREET, ALLENTOWN, PA.

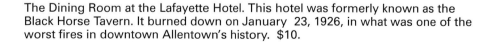

The Dining Room at the Lafayette Hotel. This hotel was formerly known as the
Black Horse Tavern. It burned down on January 23, 1926, in what was one of the
worst fires in downtown Allentown's history. $10.

The Hotel Penn on the northeast corner of North Seventh and Linden
Streets. $15.

The Hotel Traylor at Fifteenth and Hamilton Streets opened in 1917. $5.

The American Hotel at Sixth and Hamilton Streets was torn down to make way for the Americus Hotel, which cost over $ 2.5 million to build, and opened in 1928. It still stands today. $10.

The Hotel Lenox at 34-36 North Eighth Street. $10.

6. Restaurants

Pennsylvania "Dutch" food was hearty and filling, making it an important part of the Pennsylvania German experience. Heavy vegetable soups and stews were served with "filling" made from bread stuffing, thick gravies, puddings, and delicious local sharp cheddar cheese. Other local favorites were cooked dandelion greens, bacon salad dressing, chicken with waffles, and shoofly pies made from heavy molasses in several styles depending on their density. The densest was called a wet-bottom shoofly pie and the drier versions had a more crumbly filling.

In the late 1890s, Allentown families customarily walked in the downtown shopping district on Saturday nights and window-shopped. Bowen Grocers, a Hamilton Street merchant, sent out venders to roast fresh peanuts on the streets. Before long, Allentown became known as "the Peanut City" and it was said that so many peanuts were eaten by Sunday morning that the streets literally crunched underfoot with peanut shells.

The neighboring towns of Easton and Reading also had nicknames that reflected local food tastes. Easton was known as the "fish city" because of its location on the Delaware River and the popularity of its annual spring shad festival. Fishermen set up outdoor fires and cooked their fish and its roe on wooden planks. Reading was closer to the heart of the Pennsylvania German communities and was called the "pretzel city" for the popularity of its special pretzels. One unique favorite was an oversized, hard, and crunchy pretzel that was served with sweet and sour German-style mustard. The well known Philadelphia street snack, a soft pretzel, is a variation of Pennsylvania German pretzels.

Other Pennsylvania German food favorites include corn fritters, sweet and sour chow chow (a unique relish made with pickled vegetables), baked beans, and sauerkraut.

When Allentonians went out for a meal in the early 1900s, they ordered baked beans, bologna, sausages, scrapple, and pork. For the most part, it was good, solid, and simple home-style cooking.

At the turn of the twentieth century, a popular downtown restaurant was Glick's, at Seventh and Hamilton Streets. Among the most popular items on its menu were baked beans cooked in oyster broth, oysters, oyster stew, and cherrystone clams or crabmeat served in browned butter. Few Allentonians could go to Glick's and not order their baked beans.

Oysters were a popular delicacy in the nineteenth and twentieth centuries, and were consumed in inland communities such as Allentown in massive quantities. Allentown's extensive rail network made it possible for oysters packed on ice to reach Allentown within a day, and so be still fresh. When the yards of old downtown homes were excavated, builders often uncovered piles of oyster shells that had been discarded and buried. They were evidence of many oyster feasts.

Haas's Metropole Café, at 837 Hamilton Street, was well known for both its food and décor. For years, there was an eight-foot white rabbit standing in front of the restaurant. Haas's Metropole Café was a beloved downtown landmark and the rabbit mascot was a play on the owner's name. Haas, in Pennsylvania German dialect, means "rabbit." In another irony, Haas's first name was Harvey. The café had an electric sign above the door with white rabbits running around in a circle. When the sign was lit up at night, it looked like the rabbits were hopping around. When the café closed, the giant white rabbit was sold to a Real Estate company that placed it outside one of its developments near Philadelphia. Harvey Haas also owned Haas's Chocolate Shop, which was located further up Hamilton Street.

Another popular restaurant of the day was Tallman's Café, at 632 Hamilton Street. This café looked like a typical, old-style, German beer hall, or " Rathskeller." The bar was an especially fine example of this Germanic décor and the façade had timbers and stucco with German-style lamps and fixtures.

Oscar Tallman also owned Tallman's New Café, at Ninth and Hamilton Street, the former site of the Berkemyer and Keck Printing Company. After Tallman closed this cafe, a Chinese restaurant, called Rube's, moved in on the second floor. The late John Y. Kohl, a former Allentown *Morning Call* columnist, remembered that the sign over the Tallman's men's room read, "Old Point Comfort."

One of the most popular downtown restaurants in the 1960s was the Patio Room at Hess's, that served the best and biggest strawberry pies imaginable. The Patio Room was both a child's and an adult's delight. Cocktails were giant sized, meals and salads were made for two, and children's meals were served on toy stoves with ice cream arriving in a toy refrigerator.

One of the favorite stops in the 1960s was the Old Ritz Barbecue, in the fairgrounds. Its specialties were pork barbeque and homemade ice cream. A favorite was butter brickle ice cream, heavy on the brickle. The restaurant also served shoofly pie, pork and sauerkraut, chicken and waffles, chicken pot pie, noodles, bacon dressing, dandelion greens, and apple dumplings (a local variation of baked apple, in which the apple is wrapped and baked in a sweet pastry dough and served with warm milk).

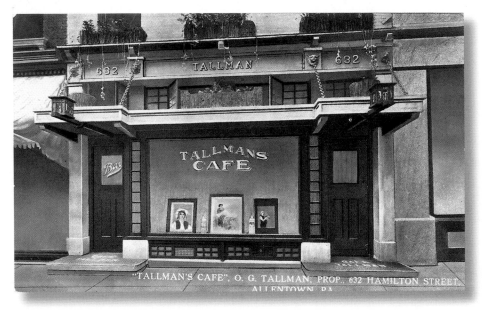

Tallman's Café at 632 Hamilton Street was designed to look like a typical old style German beer hall. The bar was an especially good example of Germanic décor. $20

The interior of Tallman's. $15.

The first floor of the White House Restaurant. $15.

The White House Restaurant at 614 Hamilton Street. $35.

The specialty at Wenner's Café at 616 Hamilton Street was pickled foods such as pickled onions. $30.

The bar at Wenner's Café. $20.

Gehringer's Brothers "Lokal" at 533 Hamilton Street. $20.

"THE METROPOLE CAFE,"
H. O. HAAS Prop. SIGN OF THE WHITE RABBIT.
CHOICE WINES, LIQUORS & CIGARS,
837 HAMILTON ST., ALLENTOWN, PA.

The Metropole Café, 837 Hamilton Street, was a beloved downtown landmark and the big white rabbit standing at the door was a play on the owner's name, Haas, which in Pennsylvania German means Rabbit. An electric sign decorated with white rabbits hung above the door and at night when the neon light was lit, it looked like the white rabbits were actually hopping around and running in a circle on the sign. $75.

INTERIOR VIEW, METROPOLE CAFE, 837 HAMILTON ST., ALLENTOWN, PA. H. O. HAAS, PROP.

The dining room of the Metropole Cafe. $60.

The Gast Haus Café at 530 Hamilton Street. "Gast" means "guest" and "haus" means "house." $35.

The Philadelphia Restaurant at 614 Hamilton Street. $25.

The dining room and steam bar at the Gast Haus Café. $25.

PRESTO RESTAURANT AND DAIRY LUNCH, 820 HAMILTON ST., ALLENTOWN, PA.

THE MOST POPULAR PRICED AND UP TO DATE IN THE CITY.   OPEN DAY AND NIGHT.

The Presto Restaurant at
820 Hamilton Street. $15.

HOME OUR ONLY COMPETITOR.   OUR SERVICE IS EXCELLENT.

CRYSTAL RESTAURANT, 608 HAMILTON ST., ALLENTOWN, PA. AND 20-22 S. 8TH ST., LEBANON, PA.

The Crystal Restaurant at 608 Hamilton Street. $10.

"ANNEX CAFE" DIRECTLY OPPOSITE HOTEL LENOX, 35 N. 8TH ST., ALLENTOWN, PA.

The Annex Café at 35
North Eighth Street. $25.

7. Banks

An early nineteenth century map of Center Square shows a bank, probably Allentown's first financial institution—the Northampton Bank that was chartered in 1814. Today, Center Square is surrounded by banks and still the financial heart of Allentown.

The Second National Bank dates from 1864. It merged in 1954 with the Allentown National Bank, which had been in existence since 1866 at Seventh and Hamilton Streets. When these banks merged, they formed the First National Bank of Allentown. In 1955, this bank bought the old Koch Brothers property.

The Allentown National Bank, which was built in 1904, was in a classically inspired Beaux-Arts office building on the site of the old Northampton Bank. The Merchants Bank, also in downtown, opened in 1903. The Allentown Trust Company, at the corner of Law and Hamilton Streets, advertised itself as the "most progressive and fastest-growing bank," but it closed in the summer of 1932. The old building was torn down in June of 2006.

One of the most colorful bankers in Allentown was Martin Kern. He arrived in Allentown in 1908, after a four-year stay at Sing Sing State Prison in New York state. Kern had a charming personality and later was variously described as an astute businessman, a clever con man, and by his own resume as a banker, an industrialist, and a publisher.

In 1912 Martin Kern founded the Penn Trust Company. One of his first important transactions earned him a $100,000 fee for arranging the sale of the Mack Brothers Motor Company. During his fourteen-year residence in Allentown, he continued to wheel and deal. He soon became wealthy and was known for elaborate parties at his Tenth and Walnut Street home. His self-promotions include earning headlines in *The New York Times* for giving $125,000 to a charity benefiting New York's neediest families. In Allentown he bought the Columbia Hotel, the Daufers Lieberman Breweries, *The Chronicle News*, and the Allentown Drug Company. As a footnote to history, he anticipated and profited from the Prohibition era's national abstinence of alcoholic beverages by buying medicinal alcohol and turning it into Guggenheim Whiskey, which he sold as a tonic at $2000 a barrel.

Kern cut quite a figure in town with his white hair and jet black mustache. He drove a Rolls Royce automobile with a refrigerator inside, filled with food and beer. Later, he earned notoriety and the life-long wrath of publisher William Randolph Hearst when he met and courted Hearst's paramour, actress Marion Davies.

But by 1922, Martin Kern had left Allentown and sailed for Paris, to keep his debtors and the law at bay. He returned to the country after a few years, lived in New York City, and tried in vain to clear his name, with the help of Allentown friends and lawyers. In 1947 he committed suicide in a New York City hotel. He had only eighteen cents in his pocket. Kern left behind a legend, and for years afterwards his name would be whispered about by old-time Allentonians who recalled his life with amazement, disbelief, and disapproval. Martin Kern was one of Allentown's most unusual and stylish sinners.

When the Liberty Trust Company was built in the 1920s at 830 Hamilton Street, the building was intended to look like Philadelphia's Independence Hall, to capitalize on its name. Although the bank closed fairly quickly, the building survived through the first half of the twentieth century, when it was incorporated into the Gernerd office building. The Liberty Trust had owned a famous mural of the Liberty Bell that was painted by Edwin Blashfield, a well-known artist of the day. The mural showed the Liberty Bell traveling by wagon from Philadelphia to Allentown, where it was hidden to save it from the marauding British armies. After the bank closed, the mural was relocated to Allentown's Old County Court House, where it still hangs in Jury Room #1.

The first Dime Savings Bank and Trust Company was located in the lobby of the Hotel Penn building, at Seventh and Linden Streets. In 1929, a new Dime Savings Bank opened at North Seventh Street,

Allentown National Bank
Allentown, Pa.

The Allentown National Bank, at Seventh and Hamilton Streets, was founded in 1866 and was Allentown's second oldest established bank. In 1954, it merged with the Second National Bank and the two took the new name of the First National Bank. $10.

DOME—Allentown National Bank
Largest Bank in Lehigh Co.

Allentown, Pa.

only to close soon thereafter, because of economic trouble associated with the Depression. This bank building was constructed with maroon brick and marble in the Art-Deco style. After the bank closed, the building remained empty for many years. Today, the building is being renovated to become offices and loft apartments.

After the Liberty Trust Company and the Dime Savings Bank closed during the Depression, the Allentown Clearing House Association arranged for them to be absorbed by the Lehigh Valley Trust Company. The Clearing House also arranged for Penn Trust Company to be absorbed by the Allentown National Bank. The Allentown Trust Company and the Ridge Avenue Deposit and Trust Company both closed in the summer of 1932.

The Dome of the Allentown National Bank. $20.

Allentown, Pa.

INTERIOR VIEW LOOKING SOUTH—Allentown National Bank
The Oldest Established Bank in Lehigh County

The Lobby of the Allentown National Bank. $10.

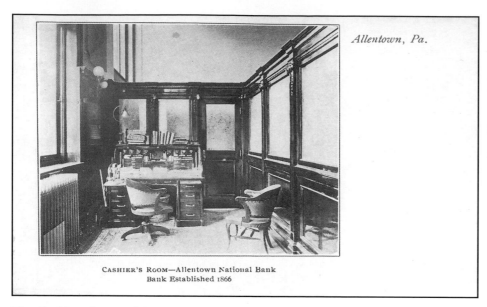

The Cashiers Room of the Allentown National Bank. $15.

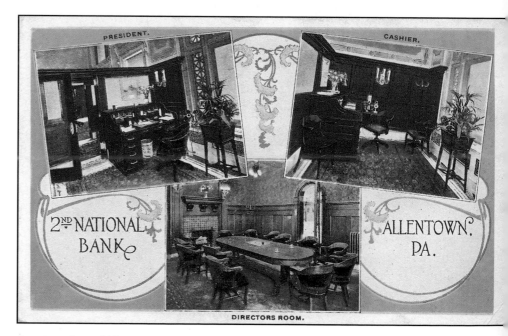

The Second National Bank below Center Square on South Seventh Street. $10.

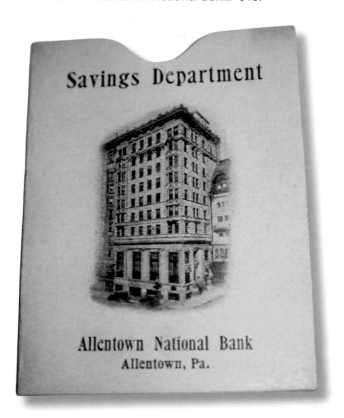

Another view. $20.

SECOND NATIONAL BANK, ALLENTOWN, PA.

Another view. $15

INTERIOR BANKING ROOM, PENN. COUNTIES TRUST CO., ALLENTOWN, PA.

The interior of the Penn Counties Bank and Trust Company. $20.

PENN. COUNTIES TRUST CO., ALLENTOWN, PA.

The Penn Counties Bank and Trust Company was in the Nathan Haas Building at North Eighth and Hamilton Streets. It closed during the Depression and was absorbed by the Allentown National Bank. $15

The Allentown Trust Company, at 523/525 Hamilton Street, advertised itself as the ``most progressive and fastest growing bank,'' but the bank closed in the summer of 1932 and the building was torn down in June 2006. $10.

The Lehigh Valley Trust Company was located at 634 Hamilton Street next to H. Leh & Company. Today the building remains vacant. $5.

The interior of the Lehigh Valley Trust Company. $5.

The interior of the Allentown Trust Company. $15

The mural inside the Liberty Trust Company was grandiose and inspiring and told the story of how Allentown saved the Liberty Bell from the British during the Revolutionary War. $5

LIBERTY TRUST COMPANY, 830 HAMILTON ST., ALLENTOWN, PA.

The Liberty Trust Company at 830 Hamilton Street was designed to look like Philadelphia's Independence Hall. The Liberty Trust Company, like many other local banks, closed during the Depression and the Allentown Clearing House Association arranged its merger and absorption by the Lehigh Valley Trust Company. $75

This is the first Dime Savings Bank, which was located in the lobby of the Hotel Penn building at Seventh and Linden Streets. $10.

Another view. $30.

46. DIME SAVINGS AND TRUST CO., ALLENTOWN, PA.

The New Dime Savings Bank opened in 1929 in a maroon, brick and marble Art-Deco style building at North Seventh Street. The bank closed during the Depression and was later absorbed by the Lehigh Valley Trust Company. $10.

RIDGE AVENUE DEPOSIT BANK, 402-404 RIDGE AVENUE, ALLENTOWN, PA.

The Ridge Avenue Deposit Bank's move to 402-404 Ridge Avenue, outside Center City, reflected the changing population shift in the city. Today the site of the former bank has become a low income apartment house. The Ridge Avenue Deposit and Trust Company closed in the summer of 1932. $25.

DIME SAVINGS AND TRUST COMPANY

SAVE A DIME WATCH IT CLIMB

ALLENTOWN, PA.

RIDGE AVENUE DEPOSIT BANK, 402—404 RIDGE AVENUE, ALLENTOWN, PA.

The interior of the Ridge Avenue Deposit Bank. $20.

8. Transportation

Allentown became an important market town because of its location on the Lehigh River, its well developed canal network, and its proximity to New York and Philadelphia. For most of the nineteenth century, the Lehigh Canal was an important and profitable business, but a series of floods in 1901 and 1904 closed the upper regions of the canal system. While the canals continued to be used sporadically, the Lehigh Valley Railroad replaced the canal system and became the area's prime means of transporting goods.

In the 1880s, Allentown had two very successful trolley (or traction) companies that provided affordable and accessible intra-city public transportation. The Lehigh Valley Transit Company served the growing population in East Allentown, and the Allentown-Reading Traction Company served the western outskirts of the city.

Through the early twentieth century, tradesmen generally delivered their goods by horse and wagon, but gradually wagons were replaced by automobiles and trucks.

Automobiles brought many changes to the area. By the late 1890s, Allentown's downtown streets had become paved with macadam and new bridges were being built to span the Lehigh River. In 1915, the Lehigh Valley Transit Company built a new Eighth Street Bridge to connect the two sides of the city and move the Liberty Bell trolleys across the river to the south side of town. The bridge was built in a direct line from the Transit Company's Eighth Street ticket office and northern terminus. The tolls were one cent for pedestrians and five to fifteen cents for vehicles. Today, this bridge is listed on the National Register of Historic Places.

A photo card circa 1890, of the Allentown Pop Corn and Peanut Company's delivery wagon. $350.

A photo card of a Gomery Brothers' horse drawn delivery carriage taken in the 200 block of North Twelfth Street. Gomery Brothers Groceries was located at 919 Linden Street. $150

A photo card of the main office of the Lehigh Valley Transit Car Company which was located on the northeastern corner of Fourth and Gordon Streets. $60.

A photo card taken on Turner Street near the entrance to City (West) Park, of the M.S. Young Hardware company's horse-drawn delivery wagon. The M.S. Young Hardware Company was located at 740 Hamilton Street. $125.

A photo card of the Lehigh Valley Car Barn, which was located across the street from the Lehigh Valley Transit Company's main office. Notice the smoke stacks of Balliet's Cigar Box Factory in the rear. $75.

A photo card of the Sixth Ward Lehigh Valley Transit trolley. $200.

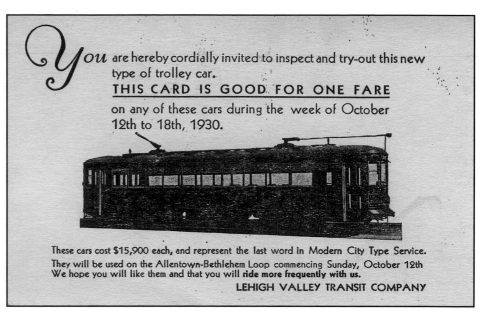

Lehigh Valley Transit Company invitational card. $30.

The Lehigh Valley Transit Company's Liberty Bell Line was a deluxe trolley that ran from Allentown to Philadelphia on the Philadelphia Pike, now known as Route 309. The trolley went from Center City Allentown through Mountainville, Quakertown, Lansdale, and on to its final destination, Philadelphia. $90.

The Lehigh Valley Railroad Station on the southeast corner of Fourth and Hamilton Streets. $20.

L. V. Passenger Station, Allentown, Pa.

Lehigh Valley Depot, Allentown, Pa.

The Lehigh Valley Railroad Station showing the three viaducts that crossed the Jordan Creek in the background. Jordan Creek ran under the station. $15.

Along the Jordon, Allentown, Pa.

A view from along the Jordan Creek. The old Adelaide Mill can be seen in the background in the rear. Note the misspelling of the name Jordon. Misspellings were not unusual on these cards. $10.

The Central New Jersey Railroad Station. $15.

An early Mack Truck. Henry Mack established the Mack Truck Company in Allentown in 1908. $100.

A photo card of an A&B (Arbogast and Bastian) Delivery Truck. $250.

A Penn Unit Delivery wagon. $200

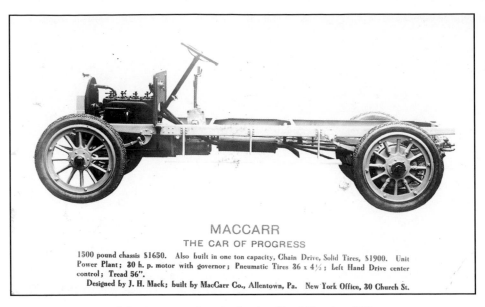

MACCARR
THE CAR OF PROGRESS

1500 pound chassis $1650. Also built in one ton capacity, Chain Drive, Solid Tires, $1900. Unit Power Plant; 30 h. p. motor with governor; Pneumatic Tires 36 x 4½; Left Hand Drive center control; Tread 56".

Designed by J. H. Mack; built by MacCarr Co., Allentown, Pa. New York Office, 30 Church St.

The MacCarr, an original automotive device by Mack Trucks. $50.

Lloyd Kline's Auto Supply Company was located at Eleventh and Hamilton Streets. $25.

A photo card of P. C. Lobach Quality Plumbers' "Bathtub-mobile." $250.

A photo card of the IXL Tire Company advertising its "Dog-on Good Service." $200.

The IXL Tire Company was located at 31-37 North Fourth Street. $35

The Keystone Garage Company was located at 519-527 North Twelfth Street. $25

The Dietrich Motor Car Company at 942-952 Linden Street only sold Cadillacs. $35

The Pennsylvania Independent Oil Company at Twelfth and Liberty Streets. $15.

9. Theaters & Entertainment

The Orpheum, Nickelodeon, Victor, Strand, and Earl are names of theaters long-gone from Allentown, but in the early twentieth century their tickets were coveted; trips to the movies and theaters were considered highlights of the week. Dancing was also a popular pastime and there were two favorite ballrooms in Allentown: Mealey's Auditorium was downtown and Al Dorn, later renamed the Castle Garden, was at Dorney Park. Until they closed in the 1950s, both attracted big bands and enthusiastic crowds.

Like many American small towns, Allentown was a home-centered society with few pretensions. The Pennsylvania Germans stressed the value of hard work, prudence, and family. They scorned frivolous pursuits, but after the Civil War there were cultural stirrings.

Allentown's first theater, the Hagenbach Opera House, opened in 1870 with a seating capacity for 1500. At its opening gala on December 28, 1870, its production, "Zoe, the Beautiful Cuban Sylph and Her Great New York Company, Brass Band and Unique Orchestra," was enthusiastically received. The theater survived for fifteen years. In 1885, the building was bought by Bowen Grocers, who transformed it into a grocery store. For years, Bowen customers marveled at the store's ornate façade, elaborate interior, and imposing central staircase which wound to the second floor.

The Academy of Music, built in the 1880s at Sixth and Linden Streets, also had a short life. It burned to the ground in one of the many downtown fires. The site is now home to *The Morning Call* newspapers.

In 1896, Central Market Hall was built on Sixth and Court Streets, between Hamilton and Linden Streets. The building was converted into a theater in 1899, by the architectural firm of J.B. McElfatrick. It was renamed the Lyric Theatre. Today this is one of only a dozen famous McElfatrick designs still standing. This strangely cobbled building, with an ornate front façade, was one of the leading burlesque halls in the northeast for many years.

In 1906, another vaudeville theater, the Orpheum, was built on Sixth Street next to the Lyric. The Orpheum was another legitimate theater and featured vaudeville and other live acts. It survived through the early 1950s, when it and the Hotel Germania, on South Seventh and Walnut Streets, were the first downtown buildings bought by the new Park and Shop system and turned into parking lots.

With the loss of the Orpheum, the only Sixth Street theater to survive was the Lyric. Since its founding, the Lyric Theatre has been the site of vaudeville, burlesque, legitimate theater, and an out-of-town, pre-Broadway, try-out venue. Since the 1950s, when it was bought by the Allentown Symphony, the Lyric has been known as Symphony Hall. In the twenty first century, after many years of under-utilization, the symphony's new and energetic board has built an addition, refurbished the interior, added new seating, and made the Hall a magnet for area musicians. Its third floor is rented out regularly to local musical organizations; the Hall once again has a busy calendar.

Today, the Lyric/Symphony Hall, together with the Allentown Art Museum and the Baum School of Art, are working together to reestablish an arts presence downtown. Under the leadership of the late Bernard Berman, a past-president of the Art Museum, and Nancy Berman, his niece and the daughter of his late brother Philip, a mural was painted on the exterior of Symphony Hall, facing a pocket arts park on land that had formerly been a city parking garage.

Vaudeville and movies, particularly the "oaters" —cowboys and Indian movies, were the popular entertainments in Allentown in the early twentieth century. Many old-time Allentonians remember and list all the theaters clustered around Hamilton Street, and the other downtown neighborhoods.

The first movie theater, the Nickolette, was built in 1907; it later became the Victor Theatre. Locals recall a big cat sitting in the ticket booth of the Victor Theatre, because the place was full of rats. As you watched the movies, you might feel a rat or the cat scurrying past your feet.

The Lyceum Theater was at Tenth and Hamilton Streets, the Hippodrome was between Sixth and Seventh Streets on Hamilton Street, and the Earl and the Strand theaters were located side by side on Hamilton Street. The Capitol, at Tenth and Hamilton Streets, showed talkies, including the first run of "Ben Hur."

Another theater, the Pergola, at Ninth and Hamilton Streets, was originally a penny arcade. It was bought by a member of the Bowen Grocery family and became a bowling alley. Two of the newer theaters were the Rialto, which opened in 1920 at Tenth and Hamilton Streets, and the Colonial Theater, which also opened in 1920 but on the site of the former Hotel Hamilton, in the 500 block of Hamilton Street. The Colonial survived until 2006, when the city finally tore it down after years of absentee ownership left it in ruins. It became a symbol of the demise of downtown Hamilton Street.

In the 1980s, Anna Rodale, of the Rodale Press family, envisioned what would be a short-lived downtown renaissance. She built a restaurant, established a design center, and founded a bookstore on Linden Street. She bought the old Church at the corner of Ninth and Linden Streets for her grandson David, who converted the 1905 building into an up-to-date theater. David named his new company, the Free Hall Theatre Company, after a theater company that had flourished in Allentown during the nineteenth century. David Rodale ran his new theater successfully for several years, until his tragic and early death.

The theater was renamed the J. I. Rodale Theatre, in memory of Anna's husband, J. I. Rodale, founder of Rodale Organic Farm and Rodale Press. J. I. was a prolific playwright and often produced his own plays at the Masonic Temple, on Fifteenth and Hamilton Streets. For several years, the Rodale Theatre, which became the Pennsylvania Stage Company, received national recognition and attracted many New York actors. After ten years, mismanagement doomed the theater and it closed its doors in the 1990s.

"Lyric Theatre",   Allentown, Pa.

Marguerite

The old Lyric Theatre, at Sixth and Linden Streets, was originally a vaudeville house. It later became an out of town pre Broadway stop for shows heading to New York. Later it became a burlesque theater. Today it is called Symphony Hall and it is the home of the Allentown Symphony. $15.

ORPHEUM, ALLENTOWN, PA.

A photo card of the Franklin Theatre at 425-429 Tilghman Street between Fifth and Sixth Streets. It later became the Jeannette Theatre. $175.

The Orpheum Theatre was near the Lyric at Sixth and Linden Streets and advertised that it showed "refined" vaudeville. Today that site is a parking lot on the southeast corner of Sixth and Linden Streets. $15.

60X230 FEET FLOOR SPACE

W. J. MEALEY'S AUDITORIUM, 423-427 HAMILTON STS., ALLENTOWN, PA.   106488

Mealey's Auditorium at 423-427 Hamilton Street, was torn down in the late 1950s to make way for the new City Hall which was completed in 1960. But in the 1920s Mealey's was a popular dance hall where a dozen dance lessons cost two dollars. $20.

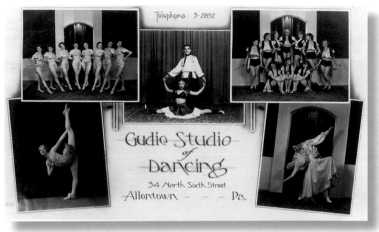

The Gudie Dance Studio at 34 North Sixth Street. $45.

Lehigh Country Club, Allentown, Pa.

The original Lehigh Country Club was built on Club Avenue on the border between Allentown and Bethlehem. $10.

10. Central Park

The development of both Central Park to the east of Allentown and Dorney Park to the west of the city were the result of vision and ambition by owners of the two area trolley companies, Lehigh Valley Transit Company that owned Central Park and Allentown Reading Traction Company that owned Dorney Park.

When Central Park opened in 1895, it was an outdoor resort offering picnic and leisure recreation for families. It remained in business until 1950. Central Park had attracted large crowds and many mothers thought it was safe for young children because it had no water access. Among its attractions were the Manhattan Hotel. The Morton Comic Opera Company, which began in 1901, performed light operas and Gilbert and Sullivan operettas at the park. Two roller coasters, the Derby Racer and the Skyclone, and a miniature railroad thrived. Rides included Shoot the Chutes, The Frolic, and The Rigamarole. Central Park also boasted a Carousel with four horses across and an Electric Fountain, which was a big curiosity in the early days.

The Derby Racer, which got its name because its two cars raced side by side, like a horse derby, was built in 1912 at a cost of $50,000. It was the park's oldest roller coaster, more beloved than the newer, 1927, Skyclone.

Central Park was founded in 1895 and closed in 1950. Many mothers thought it was a safer place than Dorney Park for young children since there was no water, no fishing streams, no swimming lake and no boating. Its famous roller coaster, the Sky Clone, was completed in 1927. $5.

Entrance to Central Park, ALLENTOWN, Pa.

The entrance to Central Park. $10.

The manager's office at Central Park. $25.

A view of the entrance of Central Park at night. $200.

The Derby Racer, Central Park's oldest and most beloved roller coaster, was built in 1912 at a cost of $50,000. $25.

A photo card of Central Park. $125

A photo card of Central Park. $100.

A photo card of the Skyclone, Central Park's most famous roller coaster, which was opened in 1927. $25

The Rigamarole, another ride at Central Park. $15.

The carousel at Central Park. $75.

The miniature railroad at Central Park. $25.

The Frolic at Central Park. $30.

The sand pit near the Carousel building at Central Park. Although most of the sand pits was destroyed, a little bit of its foundation still remains. $15.

`Shoot the Chutes' another ride at Central Park. $45.

The Penny Arcade at Central Park. $175.

The midway at Central Park. $150.

An automobile show in the ballroom at Central Park, c. 1928. $100.

A photo card of the photo gallery at Central Park. $60.

The Pavilion at Central Park. $10.

A performance of Gilbert and Sullivan's ``The Mikado,'' by the Morton Comic Opera Company which provided regular entertainment at the Park for many years beginning in 1910. $15.

The Vaudeville Theater at Central Park. $10.

A photo card of the All Clown Band. $20.

A photo card of Lee Morris, Clown of Clowns. $25.

The drinking fountains at Central Park. $10.

The Electric Fountain at Central Park. $10.

11. Dorney Park

Dorney Park's history is linked with the visions of two men, Solomon Dorney and Jacob Plarr. Dorney was the first man to see the recreational possibilities of the 279 acres of farmland that his grandfather, Daniel Dorney, had bought in 1774. In 1860, Soloman Dorney built fish ponds, or "weirs," to raise and market trout; he called it the Fish Weir and Summer Resort. By 1870 he had added lawn games, a small zoo, a few mechanical rides, and a garden area; in 1884 he renamed it Dorney's Trout Ponds and Summer Resort. Next, Dorney converted an old farmhouse in the middle of the park to a hotel, known as The Mansion House. He also added a restaurant, which featured fresh fish and duck dinners. The fish came from the Dorney fish ponds and the ducks were supplied by Gernerd's duck farm, one of the stops on the trolley route from Allentown. Dorney and his family lived in The Mansion until his death in 1901.

By the late 1880s, this popular resort attracted people to picnic, fish, go boating, and enjoy its rural beauty. Within the next few years, Dorney added bowling alleys, pony rides, and billiards. In 1899, the Allentown Kutztown Traction Company created a double track trolley from Allentown to Kutztown with a stop at Dorney Park. Round trip fare was five cents.

Eventually, the hotel moved to another farmhouse on the outskirts of the park, to the right of the entrance, and the Mansion became a penny arcade. It survived until recently, when it was torn down, despite controversy about its historical value.

The new hotel became The Hotel at Dorney Park. When the restaurant also moved to the new hotel, it became a year-round facility called the Dorney Park Inn, because it was now outside the park. By the late 1960s, the Inn had become The Mandarin House, a Chinese restaurant.

In 1901 owners of the Allentown Reading Traction Company bought the park from Solomon Dorney before he died. The new trolley service helped promote the park and enabled people from town to easily reach the park. Soon, Dorney Park became a major attraction for people from as far away as Philadelphia and New York City.

In 1901, Oliver Dorney, Solomon's son, partnered with Jacob Plarr, an Alsatian immigrant living in Philadelphia who had set up a concession and brought a Dentzel carousel with 32 hand-carved animals. They set up the park's first merry-go-round. It was a great success and Plarr and Dorney added more ride concessions in 1907, influencing the park to become known as a ride and amusement center.

Within few more years, a scenic railway was added, which was a precursor to the roller coaster. In 1915, the swimming pool, casino, and roller skating rink were built. By 1923, a ride called The Whip, a roller coaster, and a children's play area. were added.

In 1923, Bob Plarr, Jacob's son, became president of the Dorney Park Coaster Company. In 1927, the company built the Mill Chute, which was also known as the Tunnel of Love, and an open-air dance and entertainment pavilion called Al-Dorn (Allentown-Dorney). In 1935 Al Dorn was reopened as Castle Garden, which continued through the 1950s to feature leading entertainers in the country.

A late-1960s addition was a new mascot, AlFunDo, a large welcoming clown figure that stood at the entrance of the park. Its name was a combination of the words Allentown Fun at Dorney, and it was the result of a city-wide contest to name the clown.

Dorney Park remained a family business until 1985, when Bob Plarr's son-in-law and daughter, Bob and Sally Ott, sold it. In 1992, the park was bought by Cedar Fair L.P., of Sandusky, Ohio. Dorney Park is now known as Dorney Park and Wildwater Kingdom, one of the largest and best-known amusement centers in the country.

The entrance to Dorney Park. $10.

The Springs and Drinking fountain at Dorney Park. $15.

A photo card of Dorney Park's Casino building which collapsed one night after a heavy snow-storm from the weight of the snow on its roof. $200.

The Mansion House was the original home of Solomon Dorney who lived there until his death in 1901. It became the first Dorney Park Hotel. Notice that the Jacob Plarr family is sitting on the bench. $15.

The fishing "weirs" at Dorney Park. $10.

The boat dock and railway at Dorney Park. $10.

The Dorney Park Merry-go-Round. $45

The entrance to the roller coaster at Dorney Park. $15

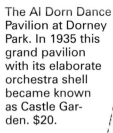

The Al Dorn Dance Pavilion at Dorney Park. In 1935 this grand pavilion with its elaborate orchestra shell became known as Castle Garden. $20.

12. The Great Allentown Fair & Camp Crane

The Allentown Fair has held an important place in local history and the memories of old timers since 1852, when it was founded by the Lehigh County Agricultural Society. The first Allentown Fair was held in the city on land bordered by Fourth, Walnut, and Union Streets. A few years later, the Lehigh County Agricultural Society bought fourteen more acres and the fair moved to Fifth and Sixth Streets between Liberty and Allen Streets. Today, only Fair Street, a short half street between Liberty and Allen Streets, recalls the fair's early existence. The fair was cancelled in 1862 during the Civil War.

In 1867, at the urgings of General Trexler and Edward Young, who were members of the Agricultural Society, the fairgrounds moved to a more spacious location on Seventeenth Street.

Trexler also helped establish Camp Crane in 1917, by suggesting that the United States government lease the fairgrounds as a training camp for the United States Army Ambulance Corps (USAAC). More then 300 medics were trained at Camp Crane that first year for service in World War I. In 1917 the Allentown Fair was cancelled once more. Camp Crane lasted for two years.

The entrance to the Great Allentown Fair. $10.

A photo card of the Horticultural Building at the Allentown Fair. $40.

The Great Allentown Fair was founded in 1852 between Fifth and Sixth Streets and Allen and Liberty Streets. In 1867 it moved to its present location on Seventeenth Street between Liberty and Chew Streets. $10.

The cattle exhibit building at the Allentown Fair. $10.

The Judges Stand at the Allentown Fair. $10.

A 1912 tinted photo card giving an overview of the entire fairgrounds including the new grandstands at the Allentown Fair. $15.

A photo card of the Ferris Wheel at the Allentown Fair. $40.

Grand Stand, Fair Grounds, Allentown, Pa.

11828

The old grandstands at the Allentown Fair. $10.

The old grandstands and race track at the Allentown Fair. $10.

The Ferris Wheel and the Midway at the Allentown Fair. $5.

The old agricultural building at the Allentown Fair. $15.

Swift and Company announced the dates of the 1906 Allentown Fair. $10.

An advertising card announcing the Fair's opening on September 21-25, 1909. $20.

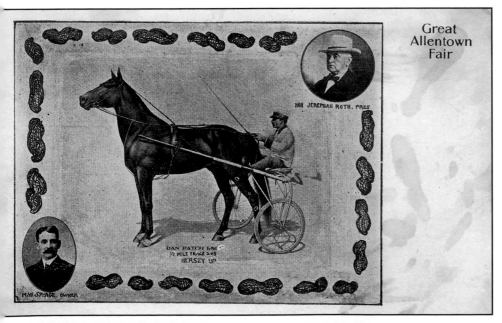

Dan Patch, the championship racer, was a popular attraction at the Fair. This prize winning horse was owned by M.W. Savage. The other man pictured was Jeremiah Roth who was president of the Fair at that time. Note the peanut shell trim design around the card. Allentown was known as the Peanut City. $20.

77

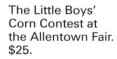

17th and Liberty Sts. | FAIR GROUND HOTEL | ALLENTOWN, PA.

The Little Boys' Corn Contest at the Allentown Fair. $25.

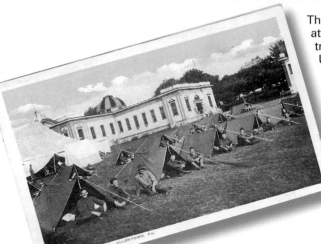

The USAAC pup tents at Camp Crane, a training camp for the United States Army Ambulance Corps during World War I. It opened May 23, 1917, at the Fairgrounds, largely through the efforts of General Trexler, and closed two years later. $5.

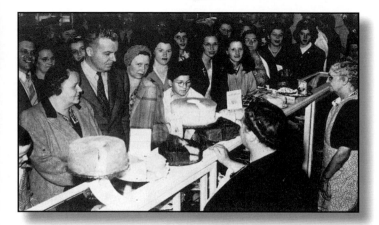

Cake Judging at the Allentown Fair. $10.

A United States Army Ambulance Corps drill. $5.

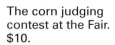

The corn judging contest at the Fair. $10.

United States Army Ambulance Corps. $5.

13. Parades

Parades, soldiers, and bands have been a part of small town culture and holiday celebrations for a long time, and Hamilton Street, Allentown, was often the scene of victory parades, holiday parades, and marching band processionals.

Allentown's militia was the first to heed Lincoln's call for troops at the onset of the Civil War. When the statue of the First Defender, a memorial to them, was dedicated in 1917 in West Park, more than fifteen thousand people gathered and twenty five bands participated in the dedication ceremony.

Allentown has had many bands and became known for band concerts and its West Park Band Shell. In the 1940s, it earned the name "Band City, U.S.A."

A photo card taken at Sixth and Hamilton Streets showing a parade about to enter the 600 block of Hamilton Street. Prior to the 1930s, parades marched out Hamilton Street. Today they march into Hamilton Street. $25.

A 1907 photo card of firemen marching west at Sixth and Hamilton Streets. $125.

A 1907 view of Tenth and Hamilton Streets showing the street before the Rialto Theatre was built on this corner. $25.

The 500 block of Hamilton Street. $5.

A 1918 photo card of a parade on Tenth and Hamilton Streets showing the new Rialto Theatre being built. The theater was completed in 1920. $25.

A photo card of Hamilton Street looking west from the monument. $10.

14. Allentonians & their Residences

William Allen's original city boundary extended from Fourth to Tenth Streets, and for most of the eighteenth century the majority of Allentonians lived clustered around Center Square below Seventh Street.

By the 1870s, the city was extending west on Hamilton Street to Seventeenth Street. During this time, Allentown began to upgrade and pave the city streets. Hamilton Street was one of the first to be paved and macadamized.

The post-Civil War era was a period of growth for Allentown as an influx of immigrants settled in the old Second Ward, around Second and Front Streets and its former residents began to build houses further out on Tenth, Eleventh, and Twelfth Streets.

The new Hamilton Street residential expansion was largely due to the energy and vision of General Harry Trexler. In 1893 he bought land rights in the West End that was beyond the city limits, was filled with abandoned open-mine pits, and had no access to public utilities. In this largely unsettled frontier, Trexler established the West End Improvement Company and soon built lumber yards and lumber mills.

Trexler was also influential in helping the city develop a city-wide park system. When City Park, or West Park, opened in 1904 at Sixteenth and Linden Streets, an expanded public park network was begun that would eventually earn Allentown national celebrity.

City Park became a focal point of the West End. Soon, Allentown's leading citizens built grand and imposing homes in this area and Hamilton Street, between twelfth and sixteenth Streets, became known as Mansion Row.

The early residential architects had few real credentials, but they got inspiration from design books. By the 1890s, architects were becoming professionally schooled and many had worked in the offices of the best architects in New York City and Philadelphia. The new home owners favored towering turrets, sweeping porches, imposing walkways, and grandiose architectural elements.

One of the early grand houses was George Ormrod's home at 1227 Hamilton Street, which was built in 1897. The house had a front and back porch, five connecting bedrooms on the second floor, a first-class billiards room on the third floor, and the rear of the house had a 100 by 60 foot tennis court.

In 1901, Henry B. Leh built Fountain Heights, a magnificent home at 1533 Hamilton Street. His son John built another home at 1537 Hamilton Street, and later George Leh built his home at 1602 Hamilton Street. Henry Leh's daughter Sallie and her husband, Horatio B. Koch, built a home at 1204 Hamilton Street.

When Henry Leh and his wife died, Sallie and Horatio Koch moved into Fountain Heights and sold 1204 Hamilton Street to Harry Trexler, who lived there until 1919, when George Ormrod died. Trexler bought 1227 Hamilton Street from Ormrod's widowed daughter.

While Henry Leh was building his new home uptown in 1901, James K. Mosser was building a house at 445 Hamilton Street. His would be the last great home built downtown.

Other Trexler uptown neighbors were Edward Young, a Trexler associate who built a grand home at 1508 Hamilton Street, and George Hersh, of F. Hersh & Sons Hardware Store, who built a house at 1244 Hamilton Street, which was later bought by Max Hess, Sr., in 1910.

A.H. Balliet, the owner of the Balliet Cigar Box Factory, also lived at 1412 Hamilton Street until his death in 1930. In 1910 Balliet bought the Past Time Farm, at 30th Street and the Parkway, as a summer retreat and a gentleman's farm where he raised rare and exotic fowl. Today Balliet's Hamilton Street house has been torn down and the Past Time Farm house and barn are owned by the Parks Department. The house is used by the Allentown Recreation Department and the barn is used by the Parks Department for storage.

Another neighbor was Martin Kern, a man with "white hair and a black mustache...and a notorious conman and swindler," who was often described by local Allentonians as a "jailbird, financier, and socialite." Kern arrived in Allentown at the age of 37, after a checkered life spent in various New York prisons for committing a variety of scams, and business frauds. But with an amazing shrewdness and social agility, he settled down in Allentown and became a banker, industrialist, publisher and even a philanthropist. His first home was at 10th and Walnut Streets near the Columbia Hotel, which he also owned. He later moved to Sixteenth and Walnut Streets.

A group that influenced the manufacturing life of Allentown was of Jewish heritage and came from New York and New Jersey. These people set up garment factories that, through the late 1990s, manufactured garments for some of the leading national brand names in fashion.

The Morris Senderowitz family was one of the oldest Jewish families in Allentown. Senderowitz owned the Royal Manufacturing company that made underwear. Like other wealthy merchants and business leaders in town, Senderowitz built a grand home at 1801 Hamilton Street, and although it had a Hamilton Street address, it actually faced Eighteenth Street.

In 1916, after touring Europe and being impressed with their city designs, Mayor Reichenbach started another downtown Allentown tradition by placing flowers in the street lights that lined Hamilton Street.

In 1917, the opening of the Hotel Traylor marked the first commercial intrusion on Hamilton Street. Located at the corner of Fifteenth and Hamilton Streets, the Traylor promised the latest in modern style and luxury, as well as a sky lounge on the top floor.

In 1926, the ultra modern Livingston Apartments were built at 1401 Hamilton Street, next to Lewis Krause's large stone and brick mansion. The Livingston was the epitome of stylish "luxe." It had a Spanish-influenced foyer and painted murals, elegant lobby, penthouse apartments with balconies, and a rooftop garden with a grand view of the city. The Livingston attracted a prominent clientele. Its most famous resident was "bon vivant" banker William Butz, whose apartment was decorated in white and was described as "Hollywood in Allentown."

By the 1920s, Hamilton Street was in its heyday, both uptown and downtown. Under the dynamic leadership of General Trexler, the Pennsylvania Power and Light Company decided to make Allentown their home, and in 1928 it built the P. P. and L. building at Ninth and Hamilton Streets, which was the tallest building in Allentown. Trexler hired internationally known artists to help bring art to the area. These included Alexander Archipenko, a Russian modernist who designed a series of "art moderne" sculptural insets on the exterior walls of the P. P & L building.

Sadly, few of the grand homes on Mansion Row remain intact. Some have been torn down to make way for new hospitals and their parking lots. The few that survive have become offices, funeral homes, or doctors' offices.

A photo card of President Theodore Roosevelt arriving in Allentown at the Lehigh Valley Railroad Station, August 10, 1905. Roosevelt, a long time friend of Allentown Mayor Fred Lewis, came to visit three times. Each time he stayed at the Hotel Allen. $50.

A photo card of Henry Mack standing in front of his Allentown Bobbin Works. $15.

Mack and His Henry at 910 Walnut Street. This man is no relation to Henry Mack, above. And today no one knows the story behind this unique bit of historic whimsy. $50.

A photo card of the Allentown Band standing in front of the Sailors and Soldiers Monument at Center Square. The Allentown Band dates back to 1852 when Amos Ettinger formed a band with 25 local musicians. The Pioneer Band dates back to 1909, and in 1914, the Jacob Max family created the first Jewish Band. $25

The 1912 Ormrod Family reunion at the Matcham Residence, at 1727 Hamilton Street. Margaret Matcham was the daughter of George Ormrod, who was one of General Trexler's partners in the Lehigh Portland Cement Company. After the Matchams built this house in 1904, they hosted all the Ormrod family get togethers. Mr. Matcham must have taken this family portrait, because he is the only member of the family not in the picture. $15.

A photo card of the Ladies Band of Allentown which was formed in 1914. $15.

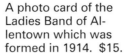

John and Fan Saeger lived in this house at Fourth and Walnut Street. The Saegers owned the Saeger Milling Company. Fan was the daughter of George Ormrod and a sister of Margaret Ormrod Matcham. $30.

Lewis Krause made his money in the shoe business and then built a large stone and brick mansion at 1401 Hamilton Street next to the Livingston Apartments. Today the house is gone and there is a parking lot where the Krause house once stood. $10.

When Henry Leh and his wife died, Horatio B. Koch and his wife Sallie sold this home at 1204 Hamilton Street to General Trexler. Trexler remained in this home until 1919, when his old partner George Ormrod died and Trexler bought the Ormrod home at 1227 Hamilton Street from Ormrod's daughter, Kate Whitaker. $10.

Homes on the south side of Fourteenth and Franklin Streets, just below Hamilton Street. So many large homes were built on Hamilton Street in the early 1900s, that the street was nicknamed Mansion Row. $5.

Hamilton St., East of N. 16 St., Allentown, Pa.

216353

Hamilton St. looking East from 17th St., Allentown, Pa.

A 1940s view of the Gernerd House at 1519 Hamilton Street at the corner of Fulton Street. $5.

The Matcham House, at 1727 Hamilton Street near Eighteenth Street. Margaret Ormrod married Charles Matcham and they built this house in 1904. Albert Gomery, of Gomery Grocers, bought the house after Matcham died. $5.

HAMILTON STREET, RESIDENCE DISTRICT, ALLENTOWN, PA.

Fountain Heights, Henry Leh's house at 1533 Hamilton Street. After he and his wife died, their daughter Sallie and her husband Horatio B. Koch moved into the house. John Leh built a house at 1537 Hamilton Street, between Sixteenth and Fulton Streets. $10.

1717 Hamilton Street was built by William D. Schantz. It was later bought by Stanley Flach who was known as a local bon vivant. $75.

A photo card of the Morris Senderowitz home on 1801 Hamilton Street. This house had a Hamilton Street address but it actually faced Eighteenth Street. Presumably Hamilton was a better address than Eighteenth Street. $20.

A photo card of District Attorney Warren K. Miller's house at 248 North Fourth Street on the corner of Chew Street. $20.

A photo card of a home on Seventeenth and Linden Streets. $40.

A photo card of ``The Cedars,'' the home of Hamilton Street jeweler Herbert Keller at 3001 Turner Street. Herbert was the son of the founder of E. Keller and Sons. $60.

A photo card of South Thirteenth Street. $10.

A photo card of the John Trexler House in East Allentown. Trexler owned the Trexler Lime Kilns which were on the east side of the Lehigh River just north of the Hamilton Street Bridge. $20.

A photo card of 1417, 1419, and 1421 Linden Street near the corner of Franklin Street. $60.

87

I received your letter and will answer it after anniversary, as I expect to see you then. Well How is school yet? I am only having a few just now. So many are sick. This is a photo of our home. We live in the one I marked and my brother lives in the other one. Good by till Sat. With Love Sophia

A photo card of 115 South Jefferson Street. $15.

M.A. Reinsmith was an important residential builder and he built many of the homes in the new Hamilton Park residential area as well as those in Muhlenberg Manor. $20.

Hamilton Park. $5.

Muhlenberg Manor. $30.

M. A. REINSMITH
CHOICE
HOMES & LOTS
General Insurance
Rooms 19-20, B. & B. Bldg.
6th & Ham'l Sts.
ALLENTOWN, PA.

ONE OF THE "CASSONE-BILT" HOMES AT MUHLENBERG MANOR, ALLENTOWN, PA.

Square, City Streets, & the Sailors and Soldiers Monument

Center Square in 1762 as the focal point [in]spired by William Penn's plan for Philadel[phia ex]tending east to west, from (what is now) [and] north to south, from (what is now) Liberty

after his family and friends. Allen Street [S]treet was named for his good friend and [lawy]er. Chew Street was named for Benjamin [a] Court Judge. Gordon Street was named [for a go]vernor. These names are still used. Allen [named for his] children, and many have been changed [Lo]w Street became Linden Street. John [and] William Street became Sixth Street; and [a] Street. He named two other streets after [his daughter] Ann. Both of these have been renamed. [one] is Fifth Street.

[leg]acies of the original grid plan is one he [every] day, as the sun sets in the late afternoon, [he is] blinded by the setting sun.

[In the 19th] century, underground public toilets [in Amer]ican small towns. In Allentown these [located] at the corners of Center Square. The [men's were] on the southwestern corner. The [women's] on the southeastern corner. Allentown [was proud to be] able to provide such a public amenity, [and it was] photographed by National Geographic [in market]ing brochures by the Lehigh Portland [Cement Co]. vandalism had taken its toll and they [still] remain closed to this day.

[The monum]ent was dedicated October 17, 1899, [The] monument commemorates those Al-

lentonians who fought in the Civil War. A 97-foot statue of the Goddess Liberty was placed on top of the monument, facing east, in the same direction these soldiers marched to the train station on their way to New York and the war front.

In 1940 Mayor Fred Lewis, then in his third term as mayor, suggested building a parking garage under the monument. He suggested that access to the garage would be from the center lane of North Seventh Street and exits would be through South Seventh Street. This idea was not popular and came to naught.

In 1956, a group of downtown businessmen, led by Richard Kuhns of Kuhns & Shankweiler along with Mayor Donald V. Hoch, believed that the massive monument was an impediment to downtown traffic. They organized a movement to place the monument in West Park, along side the park's other military monuments. After a nine year fight, the idea was voted down in 1964 in a county-wide vote; the Monument remains a downtown landmark. Most of the aggressive opposition to the idea came from surviving Civil War veterans, their families, and their children.

The Miss Liberty figure was removed in 1959, because years of outdoor exposure had done considerable damage. But in 1964, a new statue of Liberty was installed with great pomp and ceremony.

A view from Center Square and the monument looking north. $10.

The Koch & Person Clothing Store is located on Center Square near what will be years later, the future Merchants Bank. $10.

A view of Center Square looking south, with the Sailors and Soldiers Monument in the center and the Second National Bank in the rear. The Sailors and Soldiers Monument was dedicated October 17, 1899 to commemorate the Allentonians who fought in the Civil War. The 97 foot high statue of the Goddess Liberty on top of the monument faces east in remembrance of the soldiers who marched east on their way out of town to the train station on their way to war. $10.

90

The base of the monument looking southwest. $15.

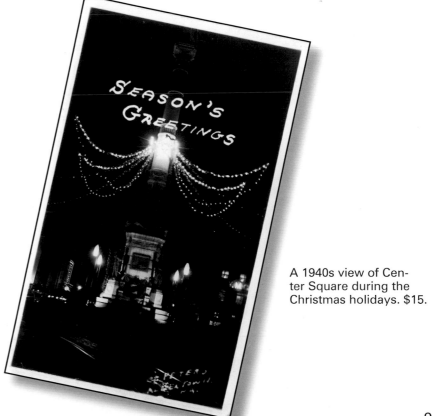

A 1940s view of Center Square during the Christmas holidays. $15.

This button was worn by people in favor of moving the Sailors and Soldiers Monument out of Center Square and relocating it in West Park. In 1964, after nine years of debate, a county-wide voted turned it down. The Monument remains a downtown landmark.

South Eighth and Hamilton Streets with the Lehigh Valley Transit Ticket Office and the P. P. & L. building in the rear. The Anewalt Building, the site of the Liberty Bell Limited Station, is on the southeastern corner. $10.

The 800 block of Hamilton Street showing the old Hess Brothers Store and the Metropole Café's White Rabbit. $10.

Hamilton Street looking west from Eighth Street. The Buckley Building, where P. P. & L. had their first offices, is on the southwestern corner. $10.

Another view of Walnut Street looking east from Twelfth Street. $10.

Madison Street above Walnut Street. $10.

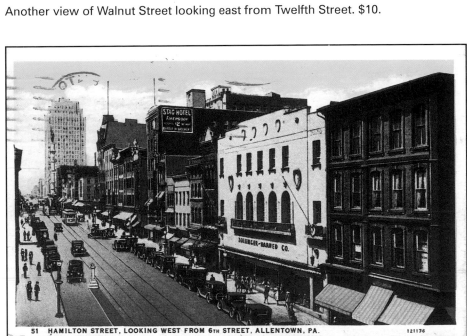

Hamilton Street looking west from Sixth Street. $5

Tilghman Street looking east from Seventh Street. $5.

16. Public Buildings

Many of Allentown's twentieth century public buildings were rebuilt on the same site or near the same location as their nineteenth century counterparts.

The first Court House was built in 1819 at the northwest corner of Fifth and Hamilton Streets. A later addition was designed by Gustavus Adolphus Aschbach. In 1864 there was another renovation, and in 1912 a final addition was built. Ironically, the building that is now called the Old County Court House was saved from demolition by World War I. Originally, the city had planned to demolish the building and build a new one on the same site, but with the advent of the War, new construction was put on hold and only an addition was built. Today, you can distinguish the additions by the discoloration and aging of the bricks.

The first Allentown Prison was built in 1813 in the midst of the downtown. In 1870 that building was replaced by a new building, also built downtown, at Fourth and Linden Streets. In the 1990s, that building was torn down and the modern Lehigh County Prison was built on the same site, towering over its neighbors. City Hall was on one side, the Old County Court House on another, and the Allentown Art Museum was behind it.

It may seem incongruous to have a jail next to an art museum, but the city planners located the prison for the convenience of both the lawyers and the prison officials. It was considered a convenience to have the Court House so close to the prison, making it easier for lawyers to visit their clients and for bailiffs to transport them back and forth to court.

The first Post Office was located in the old Compass and Square Hotel at Center Square. Later in the nineteenth century, two more post offices were built in the downtown area, one at Fifth and Hamilton Streets and the other at Sixth and Turner Streets. In 1934, the present post office building was built at Fifth and Hamilton Streets on the site that had been the nineteenth century home of Anne Penn Allen and John Greenleaf. The Greenleaf home survived through the 1920s, but was torn down to make way for a new building. The Depression dampened thoughts of new construction and the space remained vacant through the early 1930s, when the land was bought for a new post office.

The new post office building was a sleek Art Deco design. Well known American Impressionist artist Gifford Beals was hired by the Works Progress Project (W.P.A.) to paint a series of murals highlighting some of Allentown's history. These murals are now preserved in the post office lobby. One shows the Liberty Bell's famous 1777 trip from Philadelphia (and hostile British troops) to a safe haven in the Zion Reformed Church in Allentown. Another mural depicts the 1861 march of the Allentown militia to Washington, D. C., to join Abraham Lincoln's Union army.

The Commonwealth Building, on Hamilton Street between Fifth and Sixth Streets, was one of Allentown's earliest office buildings. It burned in a terrible fire in the 1950s, but fortunately was not completely destroyed and was later rebuilt.

The Buckley Building, on the southwestern corner of Eighth and Hamilton Streets, housed offices of the Pennsylvania Power and Light Company until 1928, when the company's landmark skyscraper was completed. That building still stands on the corner of Ninth and Hamilton Streets, opposite what was Hess's Department Store.

The old Allentown Free Library was located at 914 Hamilton Street, on the western part of the site of the former Nathan Martin home. In the 1980s, it moved to a modern building at Twelfth and Hamilton Streets when the city bought the former site of the Asbury Methodist Church, which had burned in the early 1970s.

"DWELL HERE AND PROSPER, ALLENTOWN, PA."

LADIES PUBLIC COMFORT STATION, CENTRE SQUARE.

The women's public "Comfort Stations" were located on the southwestern corner of Center Square. The words "Dwell here and Prosper" was the slogan of the City of Allentown in the 1920s. $15.

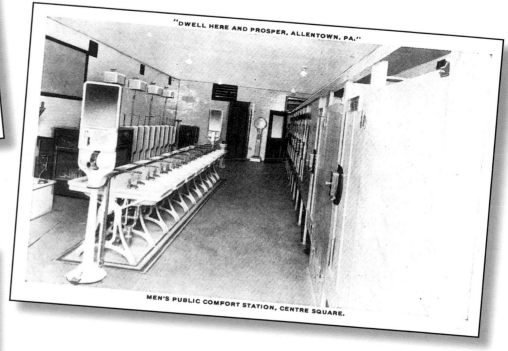

"DWELL HERE AND PROSPER, ALLENTOWN, PA."

MEN'S PUBLIC COMFORT STATION, CENTRE SQUARE.

The men's comfort stations were located on the southeastern corner of Center Square. $15.

Lehigh Co. Court House, Allentown, Pa.

The County Court House, at the northwest corner of Fifth and Hamilton Streets, is now known as the Old County Court House. The first County Court House was built in 1819. Gustavus Adolphus Aschbach designed the 1864 renovation. Another addition was added in 1915. $5.

The Commonwealth Building was one of Allentown's earliest office buildings. It was located on Hamilton Street between Fifth and Sixth Streets. It burned down in a terrible fire in the 1950s. $5.

The old Post Office building at Sixth and Turner Streets. $5.

The Lehigh County Prison was built in 1870 at Fourth and Linden Streets. In the 1990s, it was torn down and replaced by a new prison building. $5.

The new Post Office Building at Fifth and Hamilton Streets was built in 1934 on the site of the nineteenth century home of Anne Penn Allen and John Greenleaf. As part of the federally funded Depression era Works Progress Act, (WPA) American artist Gifford Beals painted murals about Allentown's history in the post office lobby. $5.

Y. M. C. A. Building, Allentown, Pa.

Allentown Free Library, Allentown, Pa.

The Allentown Free Library building at 914 Hamilton Street was torn down in the 1980s and replaced by a new Hilton Hotel. $5.

The YMCA building was located south of the Sailors and Soldiers Monument on South Seventh Street. $5.

17. Hospitals

The Allentown Hospital was established in 1898, in a building on Seventeenth Street near Chew Street, across from the Fairgrounds. The facility was celebrated as Allentown's first modern hospital. Through the years, the hospital has built many additions. The last remaining physical vestige opf the hospital, the 1940s entrance, remained visible until recently.

During the 1980s, a movement began to merge the Allentown Hospital with Sacred Heart Hospital to create the Lehigh Valley Hospital. After many starts and stops, Sacred Heart backed out and built its own modern addition. The Allentown Hospital joined the Lehigh Valley Hospital and today is mainly an emergency care and women's health facility.

When Sacred Heart Hospital was founded in the late 1880s, the small Catholic facility was located in the former home of Judge Edward Harvey. He was a confirmed bachelor and it was noted that he had a pair of ferocious dogs who roamed the large property on the northwestern corner of Fourth and Chew Streets, barking loudly and menacingly at passersby.

The Hospital remained in the Harvey house for many years, gradually adding additions. In the 1940s, a new wing was built on Chew Street. The old house was finally torn down in the 1950s, and in the 1980s a larger and more modern addition was built for doctors' offices and specialty clinics.

The Phoebe Home was originally named Deaconess Home for Women when it was founded in 1904 in the former home of Solomon Greisemer, at Nineteenth and Turner Streets. Today the Phoebe Home is a large and modern nursing home complex extending for two city blocks.

The Reverend John H. Raker founded an orphanage at Sixth and St. John Streets in 1908, in an old farmhouse, which became The Good Shepherd Home. He opened the infants' cottage in 1910 and a year later he opened a cottage for elderly people. Over the next two decades, Raker continued to buy neighboring homes to house orphaned, blind, crippled, and mentally disabled children as well as disabled and needy seniors.

Today the Good Shepherd is a modern and nationally renowned, state-of-the-art rehabilitation complex with a large campus that offers physical and occupational therapy and medical care for disabled patients.

The Allentown Hospital opened in 1898 on Seventeenth Street opposite the Allentown Fairgrounds. $5.

The Allentown State Hospital. $5.

The Phoebe Home was originally named the Deaconess Home for Women and was established in 1904 at Nineteenth and Turner Streets in what had been the home of local landowner and farmer Solomon Greisemer. It was Greisemer's son, David, who founded the nearby Greenwood Cemetery. $10.

In 1903, Milton J. Ochs built a home at 1648 Hamilton Street on the southeastern corner of Seventeenth and Hamilton Streets. Years later Dr. Harry Baer, a prominent physician of the day, bought the house and converted it into the Baer Hospital, a private hospital for women. $15.

The Phoebe Home is now a very large modern nursing home complex that extends for two city blocks. $5.

Crippled children playing baseball at the Good Shepherd Home. The Infants Cottage opened August 4, 1910. $15.

A photo card of the Good Shepherd's original Orphan Baby Cottage at Sixth and St. John Streets. In 1908 the Reverend John H. Raker founded the Good Shepherd Home in an old farmhouse on the land where the main building stands today. Through the years he bought other neighboring buildings to house the aged and physically and mentally handicapped. Today the Good Shepherd is a very modern, nationally renowned state of the art rehabilitation hospital complex. $10.

Blind, motherless children at the Good Shepherd Home. $10.

A photograph of the 1908 Good Shepherd Board of Trustees with John Henry and Estella Weiser Raker. $20.

A photo card of the Old Folks Building at the Good Shepherd Home. The original cottage for the elderly opened April 21, 1911. $10.

18. Industry & Public Works

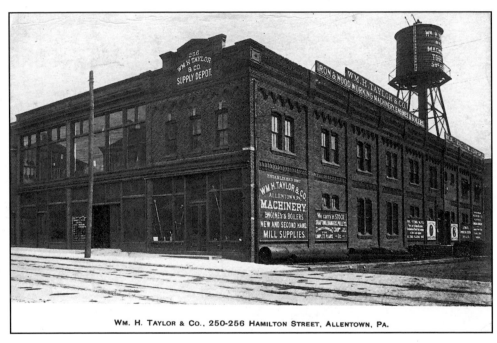

WM. H. TAYLOR & CO., 250-256 HAMILTON STREET, ALLENTOWN, PA.

The William Taylor Company at Second and Hamilton Streets manufactured heavy milling machinery. $20.

SHOP, WM. H. TAYLOR & CO.   250-256 HAMILTON STREET, ALLENTOWN, PA.

The William Taylor Company's transmission works. $15.

The Balliet Cigar Box Factory at the corner of Fourteenth and Liberty Streets. $50.

The Adelaide Silk Ribbon Mill, on the northeast corner of Third and Linden Streets, opened in 1881 to a great deal of hoopla. Many prominent Allentonians were listed as guests at the opening celebrations. The Adelaide Mill was owned by the Phoenix Mill Manufacturing Company of Patterson, New Jersey. $5.

The new buildings of the Adelaide Silk Mill were located on Third Street between Linden and Hamilton Streets. $5.

A photo card of the Allentown Steam Heat building which was located behind the A&B Meat Company below Hamilton Street near Linden Street. The building still stands today. At one point there were plans to convert the vacant buildings into a museum. $125.

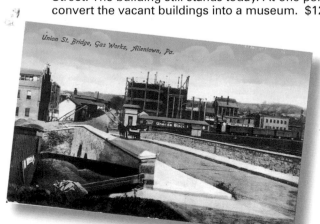

The City Gas Works at Union Street Bridge. $5.

The Kaltenbacks and Stevens Silk Mill in East Allentown. One of the Allentown mill's most famous products was the Pabst Blue ribbon. $10.

103

The Wire Mill which opened in 1880 at South Sixth and Lawrence Streets , was owned by the Iowa Barbed Wire Company and manufactured barbed wire, nails and staples until 1943. The building remained vacant for years and was finally torn down in the 1960s. $5.

A circa 1890 photo card of the John L. Trexler Lime Kilns on the east side of the Hamilton Street Bridge. $40.

The Water Works at Lawrence Street at the foot of Fourteenth Street. $10.

Another photo card of the Lime Kilns. $40

19. Public Parks & Cemeteries

Although General Harry Trexler is usually given credit for the establishment of the Allentown public park system, Mayor Fred Lewis first promoted the idea of converting publicly owned lands into public playground and recreation areas.

Tradition says that after Mayor Lewis learned of the arrest of a young boy who had broken a window while playing baseball in a city-owned vacant lot, he instructed the city engineer to look into the possibility of converting city-owned land to public use.

As a result, West Park, or City Park as it was known for years, was established in 1904 on vacant land at Fulton and West Streets, between Fourteenth and Sixteenth Streets.

This land was then on the outskirts of the West End and had originally been purchased by the Water Bureau for a future city reservoir. In 1904, the Bureau agreed to relocate the reservoir to its present location at Thirteenth and Lawrence Streets. West Park, therefore, marked the start of more collaborations between Trexler and the city.

Trexler had a keen artistic sensibility, and he hired well-known Philadelphia landscape architect J. Franklin Meehan to design City Park. Meehan modeled his park on English gardens, added an outdoor band shell, central fountain, and circular landscaped pathways. His plantings included both common and exotic trees that have become a horticultural treasure trove.

Trexler commissioned New York City sculptor George Brewster to create two memorial military sculptures for West Park in 1917. The first was The First Defender, which commemorates the Allentown militia who first answered Abraham Lincoln's call for troops at the onset of the Civil War. The second commission was for a statue commemorating the USAAC at Camp Crane. In 1925, Brewster was also commissioned by Harold MacLaine to design a small elegant birdbath in memory of his wife, Mary Ormrod MacLaine. Originally placed in Allen Park, the birdbath is now in the Rose Garden of Cedar Parkway. Ormrod was the daughter of George Ormrod.

City Park was such a success that the city created other downtown oases. In 1907, the three acres of land surrounding Trout Hall were bought for Allen Park, which opened in 1908 at Fourth and Walnut Streets.

The same year, the city purchased twenty-seven acres near Tenth and Lawrence Streets to create Fountain Park. Two years later, Allentown created Jordan Park on land that extended along the Jordan Creek to Whitehall, with the entrance at Sixth and Gordon Streets. Riverfront Park was established in 1912, at Front and Gordon Streets along the Lehigh River. This park was renamed Bucky Boyle Park in 1983.

When William Allen laid out Allentown's first cemetery at Tenth and Linden Streets, it marked the city's boundary. For many years most of Allentown's citizens were buried in this cemetery. The first burial was that recorded for Mary Huber, who died in 1765. An early stone commemorates Peter Rhoads, Sr., a local storekeeper and member of the Revolutionary-era Committee for Public Safety. Rhoads's home, at 101 North Seventh Street, was Allentown's oldest home until 1968, when it was torn down.

In 1917, Allen's colonial cemetery became Memorial Park and joined the growing number of city parks. Today the cemetery is a green oasis in the midst of the downtown and is filled with old stones with epitaphs written in ornate German Gothic script. A large plaque at the entrance of the park lists the names of those men who fought in the American Revolution and in the War of 1812.

By 1916 Trexler had built a large imposing summer home on his new property Springwood Farms which he purchased in 1901 from the Balliet family. Trexler hired Meehan to landscape 100 of its acres to resemble an English park with lagoons, long stretches of green lawn, a bridle path, a creek stocked with trout and a duck pond. Years later Trexler would bequeath this property to the city.

In 1924 Trexler became the head of the City Planning Commission and began to implement a series of connected parkways running through the city and from 1929 through 1930, he purchased lands along the Lehigh and Cedar Creek to make this idea a reality.

This project got unexpected help from the United States government. During the Depression, Franklin Delano Roosevelt created the Works Progress Act to employ American artists and artisans to create public works. And the combination of Trexler money and WPA labor developed Cedar Creek and the Lehigh Parkway's stone walls and pathways.

In 1931 Trexler oversaw the creation of the Rose Garden in Cedar Parkway, and in 1934 the Allentown Art Museum was founded in the stone farmhouse near the Rose Garden.

But Trexler never witnessed that event. He died suddenly in 1933 when his chauffeur crashed his automobile on Easton's William Penn Highway. In his will, Trexler provided that his monies be left in a trust, and twenty-five per cent of the earnings of the Trexler Trust would be given to the city each year for park maintenance. Springwood Farms would become Trexler Memorial Park in 1933, a passive-use park with vast green lawns reminiscent of English public parks. Years later cars would be banned from the park as well as picnicking, ball playing and public festivals. In 1949 Trexler's large new home was torn down leaving only the remnants of the 1800s log springhouse, and the old stone steps.

A 1910 view of the Duck Farm. The message on the back of the card says, "These would make good shooting." $5.

A 1915 photo card of Past Time Farm, at 30th and Linden Streets, looking north from Cedar Crest College. Notice the trolley partly hidden behind the house on the right hand side. A.H. Balliet bought the farm in 1910 and raised rare and exotic fowl. The back of this card lists the farm's livestock collection, which included 50 varieties of poultry, 40 varieties of waterfowl, 16 varieties of rabbits, and 30 varieties of bantams. $50.

The Duck Farm was owned and operated by C. W. B. Gernerd, and was located on the lower side of Hamilton Street near Union Terrace. It was on the Allentown-Reading Trolley Line and was considered one of the ``tourist'' stops on the way to Dorney Park. The ducks on the menu of the Dorney Park Hotel restaurant came from Gernerd's duck farm. $5.

City Park (West Park) had a band shell which was used for outdoor band concerts. The summer outdoor band concerts were so popular that Allentown became known as Band City, U.S. A. City Park was also known for its exotic and rare specimen plants and trees. $5.

Folk Dance and Athletics, Jordan Playgrounds, Allentown, Pa.

The Jordan Park Playground was very popular among the families who lived in the cramped row houses in the area. Its public entrance was at Sixth Street and Sumner Avenue and the park extended along the Jordan Creek into what is now Whitehall. $15.

Weinesberger Triplets Playground Pets, River Front Playgrounds, Allentown, Pa.

Bath-House and Pavilion, River Front Playgrounds, Allentown, Pa.

The bathhouse at Riverfront Park playground. Riverfront Park was located along the Lehigh River at Front and Gordon Streets, behind the old Neuweiler Brewery, and from its opening in 1912, it became a popular gathering spot for the area's mostly immigrant population. In 1983, Riverfront Park was renamed the Bucky Boyle Park after a popular Parks Department employee. $10.

These were the Weinesberger triplets. Their identity remains a mystery, but in the early 1900s, people regarded multiple births, such as twins and triplets, highly curious and unusual events. $20.

The Adams Island Ferry. Adams Island was not actually an island, but was formed when the Lehigh Canal was created in the 1830s. $5.

The Ferry, Adams Island, Allentown, Pa.

Babies, Mothers and Patrons at Baby Clinic, River Front Playgrounds, Allentown, Pa.

The Baby Clinic at the Riverfront Park playground. Beginning in the 1920s the city held well baby clinics at the Park for the low income residents of the area. $20

Bathing at Adams Island, Allentown, Pa.

Boating and swimming were very popular activities on Adams Island. $5.

107

Lehigh Parkway. Allentown, Pa. A4

Entrance to Greenwood Cemetery, Allentown, Pa.

GREENWOOD.

Give Your Loved Ones The Protection Of a
Greenwood Cemetery Association
2010 Chew St.
ALLENTOWN, PA.

NATURAL STONE
BURIAL VAULT

A view of the lower entrance to Lehigh Parkway in the early 1950s. Today this area is now overgrown with vegetation. Regency Apartments are now located in the right hand corner of this scene. The Regency boasts penthouse apartments with views of the parkways, the city and the P. P. & L. building which at night is ablaze with orange and red lights. $2.

2:—Municipal Rose Garden, Allentown, Pa.

A 1950s view of the Malcolm Gross Memorial Rose Gardens in Cedar Parkway. The rose gardens were dedicated in the 1940s to the former Mayor whose love for gardening and roses was well known. The gardens look exactly like this today except for the added presence of brightly painted birdhouses which sit atop the arbors and are the result of "winter busy work" by the park department workers. $1.

The portico gate of the Greenwood Cemetery. This gate stood for years at the entrance of the older side of the Green-wood Cemetery which was located on Chew Street between Twentieth and Twenty- Second Streets. David Greisemer founded the cemetery in 1898 with 127 acres that had been previously farmed by his father Solomon. The cemetery extended from Chew Street on the south, to Liberty Street on the north. In 1906 Greisemer added more acres and extend-ed the cemetery to Turner Street. $15.

This is a 1911 photo card of the receiving vaults of the Fairview Cemetery on Lehigh Street. Fairview Cemetery was considered the burial place for the Allentown elite and many of Allentown's oldest and most prominent families are buried here. It was the custom to keep bodies in a receiving vault until they were buried in the cemetery. $15.

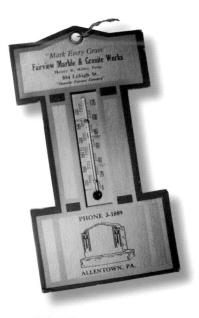

"Mark Every Grave"
Fairview Marble & Granite Works
Henry R. Miller, Prop.
854 Lehigh St.
"Opposite Fairview Cemetery"

PHONE 3-1889

ALLENTOWN, PA.

A photo card of the Soldiers Monument which used to be in Central Park until the Park closed and it was moved to the entrance of the Cedar Hill Cemetery on Airport Road. $5.

Wentz Monument Company was originally located at 1141 Hamilton Street. In the 1920s it moved to its present site at Twentieth and Hamilton Streets. During the 1980s and 1990s, Wentz became famous as a sculpture center when artists under the patronage of former Hess' owner, Philip Berman, stored marble and granite here for his many sculpture commissions. Many of these "Wentz" sculptures are now found in the Allentown parks. During the late 1980s, Allentown became known nationally as the "Outdoor Sculpture Capital of America." $35.

WOODLAWN MEMORIAL PARK — ALLENTOWN, PENNA.

The Woodlawn Cemetery on Airport Road. $15.

The Trexler Funeral Home, at 1625 Highland Street, was formerly the home of the owners of the Neuweiler Brewery. $2.

A photo card of the J. H. Romig Monument Company. $20.

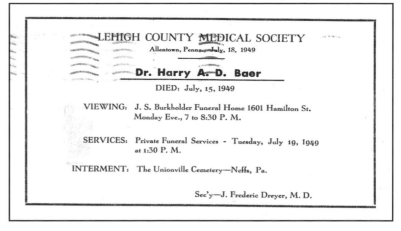

The funeral invitation card for the 1949 funeral of Dr. Harry Baer who owned the Baer Hospital, a private hospital at Seventeenth and Hamilton Streets. It was a common social practice to send out funeral invitations to the services which were usually held in the home of the deceased. $5.

20. Churches

The earliest church in Allentown was a log house built in 1762 that was shared by two congregations, the Zion Reformed Church and the Lutheran Church. In 1773 the Reformed congregation moved to a new church, and in 1794 the Lutheran congregation moved to South Eighth Street. In 1905, the congregation, now known as St. Paul's Lutheran Church, built their current Gothic styled church on the same site on South Eighth Street.

The Reformed Congregation earned a footnote in American Revolutionary history when in 1777, the Liberty Bell was taken by wagon from Philadelphia and hidden under the floors of the church, from the fall of 1777 through the summer of 1778, to save it from the British army. In 1778, the Liberty Bell was returned to its original home in Philadelphia.

In 1838, this same Reformed congregation built another church on the site and in 1886, the congregation, which is now known as the Zion Reformed United Church of Christ and the Liberty Bell Shrine, built its present church building on the same site.

In 1904 the First Presbyterian Church built a Neo-Roman styled temple with Corinthian columns at Fifth and Court Streets. This was the first English-speaking church in the area and the first church to have a full-time minister.

But by 1958, most of its congregation had moved out of the downtown area, so the church began to look for a new space. It built its present church on Cedar Crest Boulevard opposite Trexler Park.

There was no art museum in Allentown until 1936, when a group of artists and citizens led by local artist and teacher Walter Baum established a museum in the old Federal styled stone house in the Rose Garden in Cedar Parkway. The museum was offered a bequest of medieval masters from the Kress Collection in the 1940s on the condition that the museum build a modern, air-conditioned gallery space. In 1958 the Art Museum bought the First Presbyterian Church building, and within a few years, hired Edgar Taffel, a student of Frank Lloyd Wright, to build an addition that was completed in 1975.

The Christ Lutheran Church, which was built in 1903 at Thirteenth and Hamilton Streets, was the first church built on the newly expanding Hamilton Street, across from George Ormrod's home.

The First Pres-
byterian Church
built this Neo-Ro-
man Temple with
Corinthian columns
in 1904 at Fifth and
Court Streets. It is
now the home of
the Allentown Art
Museum. $20.

FIRST PRESBYTERIAN CHURCH, ALLENTOWN, PA.

Zion's Reformed Church
Here in Year 1777 in

"Liberty Bell" Concealed
Second Church Built on
This Site, Allentown, Pa.

The Zion Reformed Church,
600 Hamilton Street, one of
the oldest churches in Allentown, is now known as the
Liberty Bell Shrine. In 1777,
the Liberty Bell was taken
from Philadelphia and hidden
in the church's basement to
save it from the British armies.
This building, the third to be
built on this site, dates from
1886. $5.

A rally day pin from the
First Presbyterian Church.

A photo card of the in-
terior of the old Asbury
Methodist Church. $20.

A photo card of the Asbury Methodist
Church, which was built in 1922 on the
southeastern corner of Jefferson and
Hamilton Streets. When the church
burned down in the early 1970s, the
congregation built a new church in
South Whitehall and the City of Allentown bought the land and built the new
Allentown Public Library on the site.
$15.

111

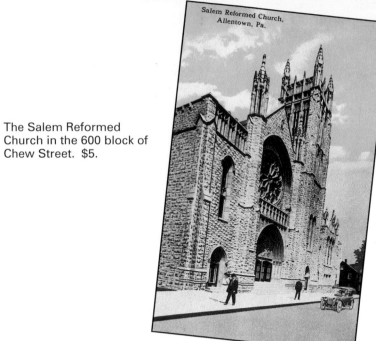

The Christ Lutheran Church at Thirteenth and Hamilton Streets was built in 1903 and was part of the new Hamilton Street expansion. It neighbored George Ormrod's house at 1227 Hamilton Street. $5.

The Salem Reformed Church in the 600 block of Chew Street. $5.

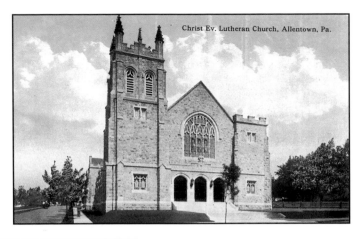

St. Paul's Lutheran Church at South Eighth Street. $5.

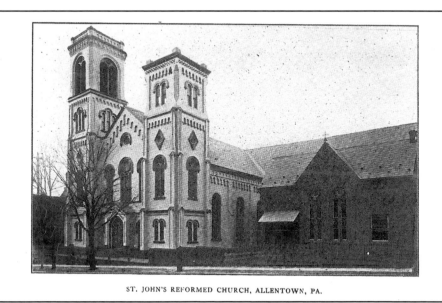

ST. JOHN'S REFORMED CHURCH, ALLENTOWN, PA.

The original facade of St. John's Reformed Church at South Sixth and Walnut Streets. $5.

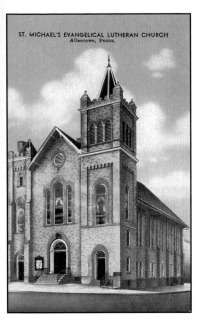

St. Michael's Lutheran Church at Ninth and Turner Streets. $10.

The First Baptist Church at Sixth and Chew Streets. $5.

The Christ Reformed Church at North Second and Court Streets. $15.

St. Andrew's Reformed Church, Ninth and Gordon Streets. $5.

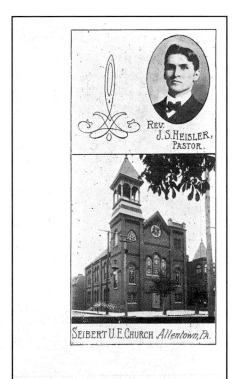

The original Seibert United Evangelical Church at Tenth and Liberty Streets. $5.

The Union Bible Class, an evangelical congregation. $15.

The Immaculate Conception Catholic Church, Ridge Avenue, Allentown. $10.

A photo card of Biederwolf's Tabernacle, a popular religious retreat at Jefferson and Linden Streets in the first quarter of the twentieth century. Biederwolf's had a seating capacity of 8000 and was the site of many evangelical meetings. During the winter of 1916, its leader Dr. William Edward Biederwolf held religious revivals and conducted what was one of the largest evangelical campaigns in Allentown's history. At the opening event there was a chorus of 1200 voices, a 75 man orchestra, an organ, and two baby grand pianos. Today the Telephone Company is located on this site. $75.

The original Allentown Rescue Mission Building at Third and Hamilton Streets. $25.

The Sacred Heart German Catholic Church at Fourth and Chew Streets. $5.

21. Colleges & Schools

Allentown's first high school opened in 1893, in an old brick building in the 800 block of Turner Street. It was the first public school to teach a predominantly English curriculum. In 1916 Allentown High School moved to a new and larger building on Seventeenth Street. Central Elementary School moved into the old building. Today Central Elementary School occupies a new building on the old site on Turner Street.

In 1963, a new Dieruff High School was built for the expanding populations in East Allentown. The old high school name was changed to William Allen High School, since it was no longer the only high school in Allentown.

Muhlenberg College was founded in 1868 when the local Lutheran Church bought the then vacant Trout Hall, and established a Lutheran affiliated school named for the well-known Revolutionary minister, Henry Melchior Muhlenberg, who was known as the "patriarch" of the American Lutheran Church.

In 1904, the college moved to its present location in the West End, and today it is a well known liberal arts school with a very modern campus and a strong enrollment and a large campus expansion including a Philip Johnson designed Baker Center for the Performing Arts, which is now the home of the college's nationally known theater and dance departments. In addition, the campus is the home of "Victor's Lament," a major sculpture by American sculptor Mark di Suvero, a gift from Philip and Muriel Berman.

Cedar Crest College was founded in 1867 as the Allentown Female College, and was one of the first women's colleges in the country. The first classes were held in the Zion Reformed Church in the 600 block of Hamilton Street, where the present church still stands. By 1869, the college had moved to a new building on the grounds of "Clover Nook," the estate of Robert E. Wright, on the corner of Fourth and Turner Streets, where it remained for nearly a half-century. In 1893, the college's name was officially changed to the Allentown College for Women.

In 1915, under the stewardship of college President William F. Curtis, the Allentown College for Women moved to its present location, originally known as Cedar Bluff, and the college became known as Cedar Crest College. Dorothy Gulbenkian Blaney assumed the presidency of the College in 1988 and not only improved the College's financial condition but increased the enrollment. When she arrived there were barely 700 students. Today, the enrollment of the College has reached nearly 1,900, and the endowment has increased from $1.2 million to $5.7 million.

Under Blaney's leadership the college acquired major art works, including sculptures of Gaston Lachaise. Three new buildings were added: a state-of-the-art science and nursing facility, the Miller Art Gallery; the Rodale Aquatic Center; and in 2004, the Oberkotter Center for Health and Wellness. The DaVinci Discovery Center for Science and Technology was also relocated to the Cedar Crest campus.

In 2006 the name of the Administration Building was renamed and rededicated as Blaney Hall.

PRESIDENT'S RESIDENCE, MUHLENBERG COLLEGE

Richard 1913

A 1913 view of the President's house at Muhlenberg College. The building is now a college office building. $15.

Berks Hall, the former administration building of Muhlenberg College, is now known as Ettinger Hall. $5

The new dining hall. $20.

1873. MAIN BUILDING, MUHLENBERG COLLEGE, ALLENTOWN, PA.

The former main college building of Muhlenberg College is now the Administration Building. After a fire in 1947, its roof was rebuilt. $5.

The Allentown College for Women was founded in 1867 and along with Vassar College, was one of the first women's colleges in the country. In 1915, the newly named college, under the leadership of its president William F. Curtis, moved to its present location, and in 1917, it was renamed Cedar Crest College. $15.

The Administration Building of Cedar Crest College is now known as Dorothy Blaney Hall after its late president Dorothy Gulbenkian Blaney who was president from 1988 until her death in 2006. $5.

Exterior views of the college buildings. $20.

The Nurses College of Allentown Hospital. $15.

The former Allentown Prep is now one of the dormitory buildings at Muhlenberg College. $5.

Interior views of the college buildings. $25.

The first Allentown High School was located in the 800 block of Turner Street, and was the first public high school in Allentown. Today Central Elementary School occupies a new building built on this site. $5.

High School, Allentown, Pa.

Raub Junior High School on Union Street. $5.

41 FRANCIS D. RAUB SCHOOL, ALLENTOWN, PA. 114018

A.H.S.

Allentown High School

Allentown, Pa.

Jackson School Building, Allentown, Pa.

The Jackson Elementary School, at North Fifteenth and Allen Streets. $5.

The Allentown High School moved to its present location on Seventeenth Street in 1916. In 1963 when Dieruff High School was built in East Allentown, its name was changed from the Allentown High School to the William Allen High School since it was no longer the only Allentown high school. $5.

ALLENTOWN HIGH SCHOOL, ALLENTOWN, PA.

The Jefferson Elementary School on South Eighth and Wyoming Streets. $5.

Jefferson School, Ninth and St. John Streets, Allentown, Pa.

118

22. Fraternal Orders & Social Clubs

Fraternal orders and social clubs were popular male gathering places during the late nineteenth and early twentieth centuries. Among the best known men's clubs in Allentown were the Odd Fellows, the Fraternal Order of the Eagles, the private Clover Club, the Moose Lodge, the Elks Club, and the Masonic Temple. The Masons had the oldest history and were among the most secretive. There were also still a few German-speaking clubs, such as the St. Aloysius Young Men's Club and the Sangenserbund, at Fifth and Chew Streets.

In 1914 the Odd Fellows Club was located in the Young building at 718-720 Hamilton Street. $10.

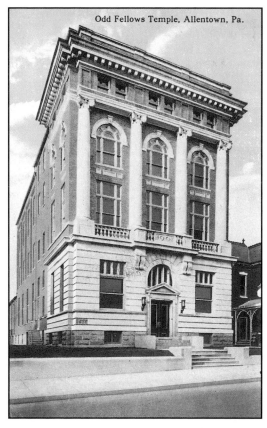

The Odd Fellows later moved to their own building at 118-122 North Ninth Street. $30.

The fraternal Order of the Eagles was located on 41 South Seventh Street next to the Dean Bricket building that housed the old Democrat and the Daily Item newspapers. $25.

The Billiards Room at the Eagles Club. The club also had its own bowling alleys. $45.

The Clover Club, at 940-942 Hamilton Street. $15.

The interior of the meeting rooms. $30.

This moose was presented to the Moose Lodge at 30 North Tenth Street. $15.

ELK'S HOME. ALLENTOWN, PA.

The Allentown chapter of the Elks was founded in 1889. Their first Club was located at 31 South Eighth Street in what was the old Stiles Building, a building that housed the offices of many local groups such as Temple Beth-El which held their religious services there before moving to Seventeenth and Hamilton Street on the site of the former Milton Ochs' house's grounds. The Allentown Agricultural Society also had its offices in this building before moving out to the West End. $10.

MASONIC TEMPLE, ALLENTOWN, PA.   112276

Vereins - Halle

des

St. Aloysius Junger Maenner-Verein,

414 - 416 Gordon Strasse,
ALLENTOWN, PA.

Only German was spoken at the St. Aloysius Young Men's Club, a German speaking club located at 414-416 Gordon Street. $35.

A 1920s view of the Masonic Temple located at 1523 Linden Street, opposite City (West) Park. Today the Masonic Temple houses offices. $10.

23. Advertising & Novelty Items

Promotions and give-a-ways have always been a popular device to promote a business, and Allentown merchants realized the value of circulating their names in the community through free gifts, such as pocket mirrors, calendars, match safes, pins and dolls. Many of these items are pictured throughout the book.

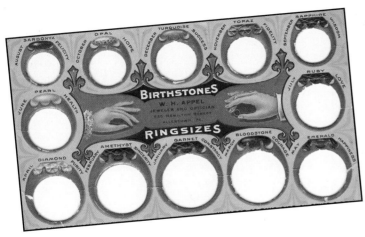

W.H. Appel Jeweler passed out this card to measure ring sizes and also suggest each month's birthstones for possible gifts. $15.

The Prince Furniture Store. $25.

Peters & Jacoby, at the northeastern corner of Hamilton and Church Streets, was a popular ice cream parlor and bakery known for its Charlotte Russe, taffy latticed shortcakes, ice cream sodas and candy. This card says, "A man is known by the candy he sends and of course it is Huyler's she wants." $15.

Koch Bros. Clothing Store. $20.

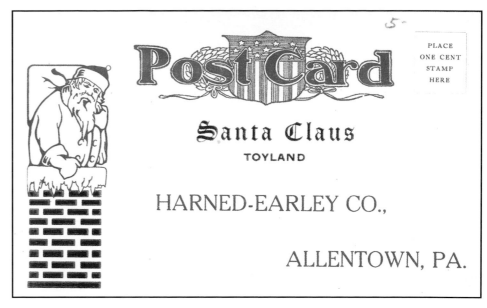

Harned – Earley was originally W. R. Lawfer and Company. It became Zollinger-Harned in the 1940s. The reverse side of the card says "Dear Santa, Bring Me." The company closed both its Hamilton Street and Whitehall Mall stores in the 1980s. $30.

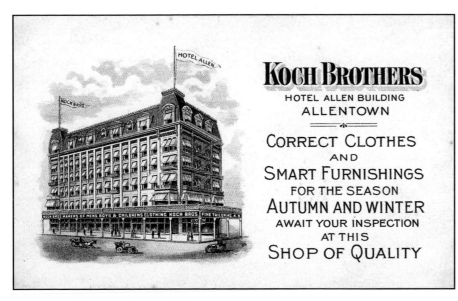

Koch Bros. Clothing Store. $20.

Wetherhold & Metzger was one of downtown Allentown's best known shoe stores and in those long ago days before sneakers became an all day shoe, almost every Allentown family brought their children downtown to Hamilton Street to be fitted for their first tie shoes. $10.

Breinig & Bachman, a Hamilton Street men's and boys' clothier, sent out this card that is dated October, 1908. It was one of a series of twelve monthly illustrations. $10.

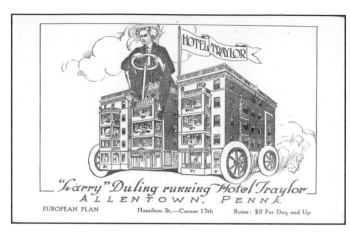

When the Hotel Traylor was built in 1917, on the corner of Fifteenth and Hamilton Streets, many of its neighbors were upset at the breech of zoning. But everyone wanted to come to the hotel's gala opening and see the new skyroof and modern designs. $25.

An appointment card used by J.M. Schwoyer, an area liquor purveyor. $5.

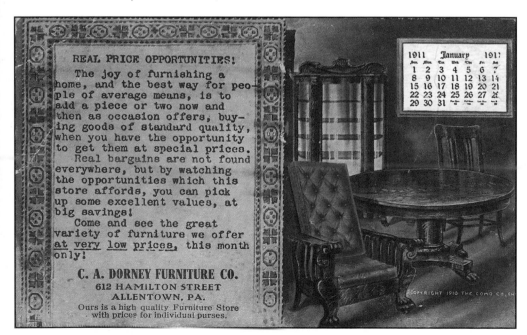

A 1911 calendar card from C. A. Dorney Furniture is one of a series of 12 monthly illustrations. $25.

A 1950s aerial view of the Allentown Park and Shop parking system. These lots were located on the side streets around Hamilton Street to provide additional parking for shoppers, but these outdoor lots could not stem the flow of shoppers to the malls. And sadly, in creating more parking spaces, many of the buildings that gave the downtown its historic charm were leveled. $10.

24. And Not So Long Ago

There have been many stores, restaurants, diners, and landmarks that did not survive the mobility of Allentown's society. In the 1950s and into the 1960s, few Allentown families had more than one car since public transportation was convenient and affordable. Stores like Hess's, Zollinger-Harned, and Leh's, as well as the many specialty shops on Hamilton Street, kept the Allentown city economy booming. Then the Whitehall Mall and the Lehigh Valley Mall rose up outside the town, and the downtown was doomed.

In the 1960s, Allentown still had a charming downtown with a friendly ambiance. But Hess's store survived longer than most because Philip Berman built a large multi-story parking garage adjoining Hess's, with exits and entrances on Ninth and Linden Streets, that kept the downtown store alive for a few more years.

In the 1970s, City Council renamed Hamilton Street Hamilton Mall and added larger paved sidewalks and benches for passersby. Canopies were built over the sidewalk in a plan to make the downtown into a pedestrian mall. But homeless people took over the benches and created an eyesore that frightened families and children away and the newly paved sidewalk areas were no remedy.

It was apparent finally that the downtown had lost its charm. The twenty-first century marked a new era for Hamilton Street, which became a financial and government center where people came to work during the day but left the streets dark and empty at night.

This section remembers Hess's Flower Shows, Pennsylvania German styled restaurants, farm markets, and the Distelfink shop, at the corner of Tilghman Street and Cedar Crest Boulevard, that specialized in antiques, arts, crafts and local gift items.

During the 1950s-1970s, visitors came from many states to see the Annual Hess Flower Show, in which flowers and plantings were on display throughout the first floor of the store. There were more than thirty different postcard views of the Flower Show. $5.

Another view of Hess's store. Notice the floral lamp posts on the street corner. $5.

The shoe salon of the uptown Wetherhold & Metzger store at 953-955 Hamilton Street. $3.

The Home Restaurant at South Seventh Street was also a popular meeting spot. $5.

Tallman's new café at Ninth and Hamilton Streets was established years after the Tallman's Café at 632 Hamilton Street had closed. $10.

Cossie Snyder's Restaurant on North Seventh Street. $15.

Tallman's new Café at Ninth and Hamilton Streets. $10.

Avondale Dairy Restaurant, at Sixth and Hamilton Streets, was a popular place in the 1940s. $7.

Zollingers–Harned Department . $2.

Van Schiver's Furniture Store was a fixture at the corner of Tenth and Hamilton Streets for many years. $1

Shankweiler's Hotel. $10.

Walp's Restaurant on Union Boulevard was known for its Pennsylvania German styled home cooking. $5.

Trexler Orchards. $10.

The Village Inn remained at Tilghman Street until it was torn down in the early 2000s to make way for a new shopping mall. $3.

The Distelfink was a popular area gift shop specializing in antiques, arts, crafts, and tourist gift items. The Distelfink bird was considered a good luck symbol by Pennsylvania Germans, and was often used in their frakturs, documents, quilts, and crafts. Other common symbols were the heart that meant love and the tulip that symbolized birth. $1.

127

Bibliography

Allentown City Directory.

Bloom, Ken and Marian Wolbers, *Allentown: A Pictorial History*, Norfolk, Virginia, the Downing Company, 1984.

Ely, Wally with Bob Ott, *Images of America, Dorney Park*, Arcadia, an imprint of Tempus Publishing, Inc., Charleston, South Carolina, 2003

Goldfarb, Myra, (Outwater) *History of the Allentown Park System and its Historic Sites*, 1989, unpublished.

Goldfarb, Myra (Outwater) *Stepping Stones into the Past, a history of Allentown's Public Sculptures,* City of Allentown, private printing, 1989.

Koch, Glenn, "Hamilton Street Mansions from Twelfth to Nineteenth Streets," *Lehigh County Historical Society Proceedings,* volume 41, 1994.

Miller, David A. and Frederick C. Miller, *Christian Miller, an American Pioneer. His Descendants Through the Families of David A. Miller and Samuel P. Miller. 1738-1956,* Privately published (and most likely printed by the Call-Chronicle newspapers).

Men of Allentown, published by Fred L. Shankweiler, Allentown, Penna. 1917.

Nuwer, Hank, *At the Crest: A History of Cedar Crest College from 1867-1988*, the Cedar Crest College Alumnae Association, Allentown, 2004.

Raker, Conrad, *Martin Kern,* private papers.

Wittman, Bob, editor, "This and That about John Y. Kohl," *The Lehigh County Historical Society Proceedings*, volume 44. Allentown, Pennsylvania, 2004.

Oral Histories

Through the years, the authors have interviewed the following Allentonians:

Philip Berman
Muriel Berman
Robert Ott
Anna Rodale
David Rodale.
Richard Peter Hoffman
Mrs. Sam Wolfe
Carl W. Appel
Mrs. Kitty Appel
Mrs. Patricia Greenawald, granddaughter of Owen Metzger of Wetherhold & Metzger Shoes
Mrs. Jill Raker Douglass, granddaughter of the Reverend John H. Raker
Mrs. Nancy Lambert Smith, daughter of Richard Kuhns of Kuhns & Shankweiler